CAMPAIGN 413

MUKDEN 1905

Russia and Japan's Battle for Manchuria

JOHN VALITUTTO ILLUSTRATED BY JOHNNY SHUMATE

OSPREY PUBLISHING
Bloomsbury Publishing Plc
Kemp House, Chawley Park, Cumnor Hill, Oxford OX2 9PH, UK
29 Earlsfort Terrace, Dublin 2, Ireland
1385 Broadway, 5th Floor, New York, NY 10018, USA
E-mail: info@ospreypublishing.com
www.ospreypublishing.com

OSPREY is a trademark of Osprey Publishing Ltd

First published in Great Britain in 2025

© Osprey Publishing Ltd, 2025

All rights reserved. No part of this publication may be reproduced or transmitted in any form or by any means, electronic or mechanical, including photocopying, recording, or any information storage or retrieval system, without prior permission in writing from the publishers.

A catalogue record for this book is available from the British Library.

ISBN: PB 9781472864222; eBook 9781472864215; ePDF 9781472864208; XML 9781472864192

25 26 27 28 29 10 9 8 7 6 5 4 3 2 1

Maps by Bounford.com
3D BEVs by Paul Kime
Index by Alan Rutter
Typeset by PDQ Digital Media Solutions, Bungay, UK
Printed by Repro India Ltd.

Osprey Publishing supports the Woodland Trust, the UK's leading woodland conservation charity.

To find out more about our authors and books visit www.ospreypublishing.com. Here you will find extracts, author interviews, details of forthcoming events and the option to sign up for our newsletter.

Note on dates

Gregorian Calendar dates are used throughout the book. At the time of the Battle of Mukden, the Russian Empire used the Julian Calendar, which was 13 days behind the Gregorian Calendar (used by Western Europe and the United States). Therefore, in the text, the last day of the Battle of Mukden is 10 March 1905, whereas contemporary Russian accounts would state it as 25 February.

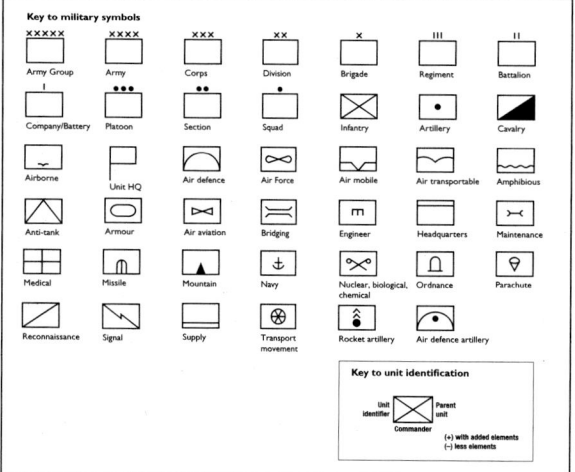

Front cover main illustration: Rennenkampf guiding in his last reserve on Fountain Hill, March 1905. (Johnny Shumate)
Title page image: Japanese infantry on the march. (Author's collection)

CONTENTS

ORIGINS OF THE CAMPAIGN   4
A land war in Manchuria ▪ The road to war ▪ The course of the war from February 1904 to January 1905 ▪ Mishchenko's cavalry raid ▪ The battle of San-de-pu

CHRONOLOGY   20

OPPOSING COMMANDERS   22
Russian ▪ Japanese

OPPOSING FORCES   27
Russian ▪ Japanese ▪ Orders of battle

OPPOSING PLANS   38
Russian ▪ Japanese

THE CAMPAIGN   42
The battlefield ▪ Phase I – Diversion, 19–26 February ▪ Phase II – Initiation, 27–28 February
Phase III – Envelopment, 1–3 March ▪ Phase IV – Russian counter-attack, 4–7 March
Phase V – Defence of Mukden, 8 March ▪ Phase V – Defence of Mukden, 9–10 March
Phase VI – Retreat, 11–20 March

AFTERMATH   89
Massing in Manchuria ▪ Conclusion

THE BATTLEFIELD TODAY   92

FURTHER READING   94

INDEX   95

ORIGINS OF THE CAMPAIGN

A LAND WAR IN MANCHURIA

For two weeks in late August and early September 1902, a great battle raged in central Russia. The Kursk province ('oblast') of the Russian Empire reverberated from the interminable firing of 400 cannon, the marching of 90,000 soldiers and the hooves of over 20,000 horses. For the first time on Russian soil, a coordinated display of military might at this scale was not an actual battle, but rather wargames, or military exercises, orchestrated by Tsar Nicholas II's visionary Minister of War, Aleksey Nikolaevich Kuropatkin.[1]

In 1902, the year of the Grand Manoeuvres at Kursk, the Russian Empire and its army were capitalizing on a long period of relative peace. Since Tsar Alexander II abolished serfdom in 1861, Russia had experienced several decades of rapid and profound transformation. Such change was not only experienced in society, but also in the foremost bulwark of Russian tradition – the Imperial Army. While ultimately successful in its last major war with the Ottomans in 1877–78, foreign observers noted many shortcomings in the Russian officer corps and army more generally, which called into question its ability to prevail against a European army such as that of the Germans or Austrians.[2] A few of the major shortcomings in the previous war were the Russians' rigid adherence to inappropriate or antiquated tactics, poor coordination between corps and, to some extent, inferior weapons. Observers believed that too many family members of the tsar were commanding armies and corps, which limited merit-based promotions at the highest echelons.

The old Mandarin highway that passed through Mukden was the route for part of Kuropatkin's army during its retreat. This is an early war image of soldiers still dressed in the summer rubashka. (Boston Public Library Stereograph Collection)

Contrary to popular modern conceptions of the late Russian Empire, there were many reform-minded officers and statesmen who recognized the deficiencies in their state and army, and who wished to apply the latest ideas on military reform, science and training to ameliorate them. Officially, the Russian high command placed more value than ever before on the 'science' of war, as evidenced by the 1896 policy of reserving one-third of regimental commands for *genshtabist* – graduates of the General Staff Academy. By 1904, there were over 1,200 *genshtabist* in the Imperial Army, more than ever

---

1 John Steinberg, 'Imperial Wargames 1896–1907', in *The Military and Society in Russia: 1450–1917*, ed. Donald Ostrowski (Leiden; Boston, MA: Brill, 2002), 259–262.
2 Roger Reese, *The Imperial Russian Army in Peace, War, and Revolution, 1856–1917* (Lawrence: University Press of Kansas, 2019), 177–179, 189–192.

before. There was an expectation that their proliferation among the staffs of Russian units at echelon would result in efficient and well-coordinated manoeuvres and cooperation among units.

The 1902 Grand Manoeuvres at Kursk were a clear sign of the growing influence of *genshtabist*. A 'Moscow Army' under the command of Grand Duke Sergei Aleksandrovich played the role of invader and mobilized to face a 'Kiev Army' under the joint command of the tsar and Kuropatkin. While the planners of the exercise could not totally shed the nepotism of the Russo-Turkish War, they did succeed in planning and executing a large-scale training exercise that included two opposing armies conducting operational shifts from defence to offense, and back again to defence. These were difficult logistical feats for large modern armies, and embodied a new, more serious approach to training.

Kuropatkin meant the exercises to be competitive and the outcome not foreordained. However, his efforts suffered from the normal Imperial Russian pathologies when aides, senior generals and guard officers used their influence and prestige to shape the exercise to meet their various vested interests, or to ensure the tsar's personal tactical decisions resulted in successful outcomes.

Two years later, upon taking command of the Russian Manchurian Army at the outset of the war with Japan, Kuropatkin was still thinking of the lessons of the Grand Manoeuvres. In a memorandum to the officers in the 1st Manchurian Army, he warned of notable shortfalls he had observed at Kursk. He noted that Russian officers at echelon rarely seized the initiative in times of confusion, and Russian scouts rarely conducted thorough reconnaissance. When they did succeed in locating the enemy, the processing and dissemination of intelligence proceeded slowly through the staffs of the various Russian formations.[3] Despite these lessons pulled from realistic training, the proliferation of *genshtabist* throughout the headquarters of the army and a near total elimination of *granddukism* (the appointment of members of the tsar's own family to key positions in the high command) in the Manchurian area of operations, Kuropatkin would ultimately lose the next war. Many of the shortcomings noted in 1902 would plague Kuropatkin's command in 1904–05. These remained salient points of failure at the greatest battle of the war and the largest pitched battle in history in 1905, at Mukden.

Stackelberg commanded the 1st Siberian Corps at the battle of Telissu (pictured) and at San-de-pu, but his subordinate, Gerngross, would command the corps at Mukden. (Author's collection)

Some Russian commanders did successfully employ cavalry throughout the war and at Mukden. (Drawing by Riccardo Salvadori, from L'Illustrazione Italiana, Year XXXI, No 14, April 3, 1904/DEA/BIBLIOTECA AMBROSIANA/Contributor)

3   Steinberg, 'Imperial Wargames 1896–1907', 259–262.

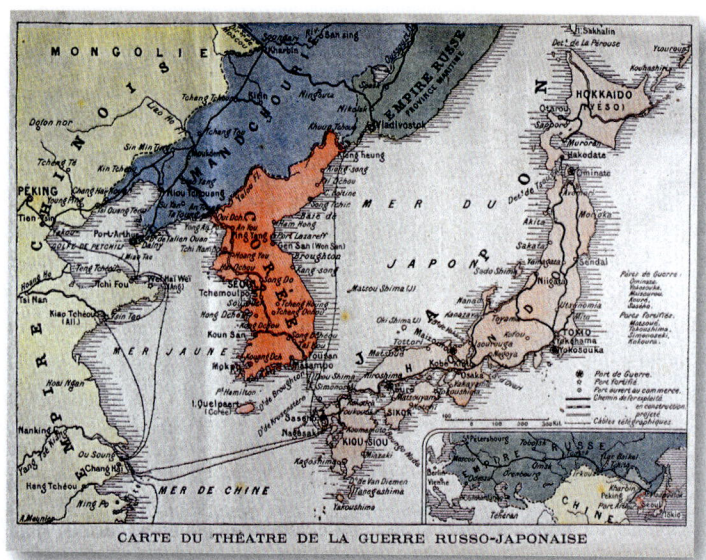

Contemporary French newspaper's depiction of the theatre of war: Japan, Korea, Manchuria (China) and the Russian 'Far East'. (Photo by Art Media/Print Collector/Getty Images)

THE ROAD TO WAR

The general expectation in Russia at the turn of the 20th century was that the next great war would be in Europe. Whether such a war would be fought against the German Empire, the Austrian Empire or to suppress another Polish rebellion (the last one of which they put down only in 1864), the Russian high command prepared commensurately and prioritized the western districts of the Empire. In the Polish districts alone, the Russian War Ministry concentrated more than 45 per cent of its total peacetime strength, some 600,000 troops.

This prioritization was especially notable in the War Ministry's concentration of railways, the ultimate arbiter of military mobilizations since 1870. In the 1890s, the Russian military built over 40,000km of military railway tracks to support potential operations in Europe, while only dedicating approximately 7,000km to all of Central Asia and the Far East. The western theatre, corresponding to the region of Poland, was given the greatest allocation – ten lines, with three of these being double-tracked (two sets of parallel railways allowing easy two-way traffic). In comparison, during the war in 1904–05, the armies in Manchuria would receive reinforcements and mobilized reserves by a sole, single-tracked line, the Trans-Siberian Railway system.[4] Operating a ground line-of-supply on a single-track line was difficult in the best of times, as two-way traffic needed to be deconflicted. In war, operations would be complicated by overuse, maintenance requirements, repairing damage or clearing accidents and, in some cases, sabotage.

Russian forces had spent the mid-to-late 19th century expanding the empire at the points of least resistance along its borders. In the Far East, the Russians shared a border with Qing China in the region of the Amur River. After some skirmishes, the two empires confirmed the Amur boundary through the Treaty of Peking in 1860, an agreement which stabilized the region for nearly 40 years. The 1860s and 1870s witnessed the final Russian conquests in Central Asia, bringing the Russian Empire into contact with the British, who were expanding out of southern Asia. The Pamir Treaty of 1895 achieved an understanding in Central Asia for the time being. In this context, rather than reflecting ignorance or negligence, Russian allocations of manpower and railway resources to Europe reflected pragmatic prioritization. Furthermore, certain high-ranking Russian officials, such as Finance Minister Sergei Witte, would eventually recognize the implicit threat that Russian reinforcements to the Far Eastern region posed to the rising Japanese Empire. By the early 1900s, Witte warned that, in this particular region, preparations for war seemed to greatly increase the likelihood of one occurring.

---

4   Bruce W. Menning, *Bayonets Before Bullets: The Imperial Russian Army 1861–1914* (Bloomington: Indiana University Press, 2000), 116–118.

Prior to the Boxer Rebellion in China in 1900, there seemed to be little risk of a major war in the Far East. The Chinese were politically weak and fatally undermined by corruption. Furthermore, the ruling Qing could be easily strong-armed into advantageous treaties if Russia needed further concessions. The Japanese, while noted for their rapid industrial development and disciplined military, had only a small army of 120,000 men in the 1890s, too small to seriously threaten even a remote part of the Russian Empire. Furthermore, to wage war in Asia, the Japanese would have to transport their troops across the Sea of Japan to Korean or Manchurian landing zones. To ensure the success of such an operation required a powerful Japanese navy, which, in the 1890s, was still incipient. Even the remarkable Japanese victory over the Chinese in 1894–95 did not alert the Russians to an imminent threat. In the view of the Russians, the Sino-Japanese War was more a testament to Chinese weakness than Japanese effectiveness. There was truth in this perspective, as the Chinese barely put up any resistance before melting away at Lüshunkou (soon to be renamed Port Arthur) in 1894, enabling the Japanese to capture this important port while suffering only 288 casualties. Russia, France and Germany's Triple Intervention further allayed fears of Japan. In this ultimatum, delivered after Japan's decisive military victory over the Chinese in 1895, Russia and the other European powers were able to diplomatically pry Japanese forces from their hard-earned conquests, forcing them back across the sea.

Sergei Witte was easily one of the most remarkable statesmen in the late Russian Empire. At first a proponent of expansion into Manchuria, he later advised caution and détente prior to the outbreak of war. (Photo by Hulton Archive/Getty Images)

Upon realizing the immediacy of Japanese designs on Lüshunkou and the Liaodong Peninsula on which it was situated, the Russians began economically and diplomatically expanding into Manchuria after 1895, in an attempt to strengthen their own influence in the region. Despite little deliberate strategic guidance from St Petersburg, Russian expansion in the region took on a life of its own as the interests of military officials and even entrepreneurs began driving events. Initially, under the supervision of Witte, the Russians secured a favourable economic treaty with Qing China in 1896. This treaty allowed the Russians to begin an addition to the Trans-Siberian system, the China Eastern Railway, a rail network spanning Manchuria and connecting Russian lines in the Amur region to the port of Lüshunkou. The next year, following the lead of the Germans and British in forcibly securing leases to Chinese ports, the Russians bribed and threatened their way into gaining a 25-year lease of the entire Liaodong Peninsula. When the Boxer Rebellion began in China, which was partially in response to these European encroachments, Tsar Nicholas II ordered in Russian troops from the neighbouring Amur District. They were able to occupy and pacify Manchuria by September 1900, and while required by treaty to eventually leave, were slow in doing so. An additional source of tension was influential Russian businessman Aleksandr Bezobrazov, who used his leverage with the tsar to gain the funds and access to build an ostensibly private lumber company along the Yalu River. This company, operating on the Korean border and frequently blurring the lines between government and private enterprise, was seen by Japan as especially threatening.[5]

In the late 1890s and early 1900s, Korea and Manchuria represented a last opportunity for conquest for both Russia and Japan. These were the only frontier territories left where expansion was conceivable without initiating

---

5   This was exacerbated by the company's practice of hiring labour from recently discharged Russian soldiers – see Corbett, *Maritime Operations in the Russo-Japanese War, Vol I*.

war with a formidable power. By September 1900, the actions of Russia would nearly make Russian dominance of the region a *fait acompli*. From 1901–03, both Russian and Japanese diplomats attempted to resolve the impasse without resorting to war. The Japanese correctly assessed that time was not on their side, as allowing the Russians to remain in Manchuria beyond early 1904 would seemingly seal the region's fate. In addition to stationing further troops in Manchuria and on the Liaodong Peninsula, local Russian officials began to fortify Port Arthur itself. Most significantly, construction of the Trans-Siberian Railway was nearing completion. This system consisted not only of the Trans-Siberian line itself, but also the Circum–Baikal line, Trans-Baikal Railway, Ussuri Railway and the Chinese Eastern Railway. In effect, this system gave the Russian Empire meaningful access and ability to quickly reinforce by land its Far Eastern possessions. Begun in 1891, this strategic asset was reaching completion by 1904. Notwithstanding the challenges of operating on an overextended, single-tracked line, the completion of the rail line would nonetheless transform the strategic landscape of the Far East.

There was, in effect, a window in time and space that was quickly closing by January 1904. Japanese military leaders and diplomats knew that they had only a few more months, or at best a year, during which Russia would be severely disadvantaged at the outset of a war in Manchuria. In this context, the Japanese initiated hostilities with a surprise naval torpedo attack on the Russian Pacific Squadron at Port Arthur on 24 January 1904.

THE COURSE OF THE WAR FROM FEBRUARY 1904 TO JANUARY 1905

Despite the impressive scale of the armies at the Kursk wargames, the battles in Manchuria in 1904–05, especially at Liaoyang, the Sha-Ho and Mukden, would exceed them many times in size and complexity. This scale would place a premium on efficient staff work and subordinate commander initiative, aspects of large-scale military operations that, while modelled at Kursk, were taxed in the extreme in Manchuria. Furthermore, certain anticipated technological developments, such as the widespread employment of machine guns, were not properly prepared for prior to the war with Japan. Lastly, war was still ultimately a human endeavour, and factors such as a commander's caution, audacity, a successfully employed deception or loss of nerve could still either ensure victory or fatally alter the course of a battle.

The Russo-Japanese War that began in January 1904 can best be understood as an extended meeting engagement, with both empires taking many months to mass their forces for a climactic fight. The Japanese would take approximately six months before their armies were successfully deployed and operating in Manchuria, while the Russian deployment would still be ongoing after 20 months. Russia was precluded from massing its superior strength by distance, decision and political will. Only 140,000 or so Russian soldiers were in Manchuria

Though they are in summer dress, this illustration gives a good depiction of Japanese field artillery in action. (Photo by Ann Ronan Pictures/Print Collector/Getty Images)

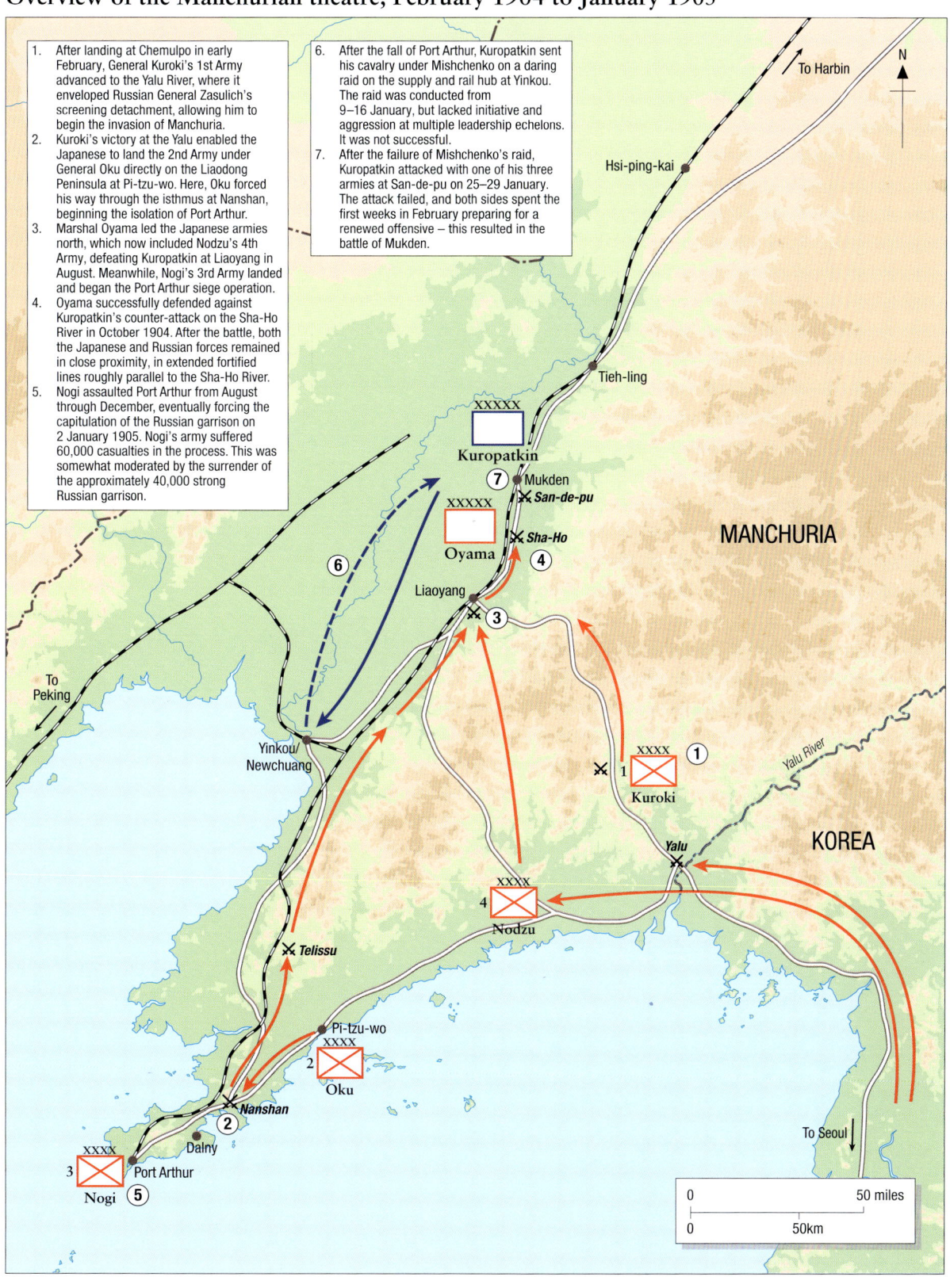

One can imagine the chaos of tens of thousands moving through these streets on 10 March in an attempt to escape Oyama's converging armies. (Syracuse University Art Museum/Bridgeman Images)

Nanshan – soldiers of the 5th East Siberian Rifle Regiment observing the effects of their rifle and machine-gun fire. (Author's collection)

when the war unexpectedly began in February 1904, while the remaining 1 million Russian regulars were stationed mostly in the furthest western provinces of the empire. Meanwhile, Russia's true advantage lay in its nearly 3 million trained reservists, who were only gradually leveraged through the course of nine waves of mobilization over a period of 21 months.

While Port Arthur was the focus of the 1894–95 war, the Japanese plans in 1904 appropriately prioritized the rail hubs of Liaoyang (380km/235 miles north-west and inland of Port Arthur) and Mukden (a further 60km/40 miles north-west and inland). The Japanese high command correctly assessed that through consecutively seizing these rail hubs, they would disrupt Russia's ability to effectively reinforce its army in Manchuria. While pursuing these objectives, the Japanese Army would theoretically need to divert only a division or so to block Russian forces on the narrow Liaodong Peninsula and in Port Arthur, where they would be unable to interfere with the Japanese main effort. Meanwhile, the Japanese Navy would fulfil its role of destroying or blockading the Russian Navy in Port Arthur, thereby preventing any interference with the landing of troops or disrupting the general course of the land campaign.

On 8 and 9 February 1904, elements of General (Gen) Kuroki's 1st Army were the first Japanese units to land on the Asian mainland at Chemulpo, Korea, later known famously in the West as Inchon. Kuroki's forces quickly made their way up to the city of Pyongyang, where he completed massing his army. On 3 May 1904, Kuroki's army forded the Yalu and decisively enveloped a Russian corps-sized detachment under Gen Zasulich, thereby beginning the invasion of Manchuria.

Kuroki's forcing of the Yalu paved the way for the Japanese 2nd Army, commanded by Gen Oku, to land at Pitsewo, located directly on the Liaodong Peninsula. Oku's army was tasked with defeating Russian forces on the peninsula and its periphery, forcing them to retreat south into Port Arthur, where they could be 'bottled up' by a small blocking force. In a bloody battle at Nanshan, Oku succeeded in this task, but at the cost of 5,000 casualties, 10 per cent of his force, compared to only 1,600 Russian casualties. While battles between armies in this period were expected to be bloody, the carnage at Nanshan was most notable as the Russian force consisted of only one regiment. Nonetheless, Oku achieved his purpose, and left one division to the recently arrived Gen Nogi near the port town of Dalny, where it would form the basis of the now-forming

Japanese 3rd Army. Nogi's 3rd Army was tasked to seize Port Arthur.

Gathering his remaining forces, Oku turned north with the 2nd Army to engage the 1st Siberian Corps under Gen Georg von Stackelberg, which was advancing against Oku's army to prevent the isolation of Port Arthur. Oku decisively defeated Stackelberg's corps at the battle of Telissu on 14–15 June, sending the remnants of the Russian force fleeing north to the rail hub at Liaoyang.

In previous weeks, further Japanese reinforcements had arrived at Chemulpo, forming the basis of the Japanese 4th Army under Nodzu. Having isolated the Liaodong Peninsula, and assigned Nogi's 3rd Army to the siege of Port Arthur, the overall Japanese commander, Marshal Oyama, was ready to begin an offensive north with the remaining three Japanese armies. Oyama ordered Kuroki, Oku and Nodzu's armies to move north along different routes that would converge on Liaoyang. On 10 July, Kuroki's 1st Army moved north through the key west-to-east running ridgeline, where they pushed aside Feodor Keller's 3rd Siberian Corps at the Motien Pass. Despite Kuropatkin's expectation that the Japanese could be blocked at Motien, Kuroki's three divisions quickly outflanked Keller's position, causing Keller to order a premature retreat. Keller was later killed by Japanese artillery fire during an abortive, six-regiment counter-attack to retake the Motien Pass.

Kuropatkin's inability to prevent this series of successful Japanese manoeuvres did not in and of itself determine the fate of the campaign. As of July and August 1904, Russian forces in Port Arthur still held firm in the face of extremely costly frontal assaults by Nogi's 3rd Army. Meanwhile, between March and July, Kuropatkin had massed six corps at Liaoyang – nearly 160,000 men (1st–4th Siberian Corps, X and XVII Army Corps). For the Japanese to seize their first of two primary objectives – the rail hub at Liaoyang – they would have to defeat Kuropatkin and his now slightly numerically superior force in pitched battle. From 10–20 August, Oyama's force of three Japanese armies achieved just that. Through a series of relentless frontal attacks by the 2nd and 4th Armies, and a bold flanking attack by the remaining 1st Army, Oyama was able to partially envelop the Russian position, leading Kuropatkin to order a retreat on 21 August. Notwithstanding the determined nature of the Japanese assaults, Kuropatkin still may have held the field had he not on two occasions lost his nerve and fallen victim to fears of additional Japanese forces arriving on his flanks. In reality, the Japanese offensive was losing momentum, as Russian formations such as the 1st and 3rd Siberian Corps successfully held off repeated assaults. Nonetheless, by the end

Kuroki's army rapidly enveloped Gen Keller's force at Motien Pass, and while the battle was not especially bloody, Keller would be killed during the encounter and his subordinate, Rennenkampf, severely wounded shortly after it. (Author's collection)

The key terrain of the October battle of the Sha-Ho would be fought over again during the battle of Mukden, four months later. (Author's collection)

This photograph gives a good impression of the cold weather clothing of the average Japanese soldier in the campaign. (Syracuse University Art Museum/Bridgeman Images)

of the battle, a slightly inferior Japanese force of around 125,000 soldiers had forced Kuropatkin's 1st Manchurian Army to retreat, allowing the Japanese capture of Liaoyang.

Kuropatkin's army retreated north towards Mukden, where it established a defensive line south of the city along the Sha-Ho River. In the first week of September, reinforcements arrived from Russia by rail, replacing losses and bringing Kuropatkin's force to a total of nine corps – almost 200,000 men. Further to the south, Oyama's armies at Liaoyang began to suffer from two logistical constraints: lengthening supply lines as they advanced inland, and the competition for replacements and supplies with Nogi's 3rd Army besieging Port Arthur. The substantial casualties both forces had already incurred in battle were beginning to strain the Japanese replacement system. Oyama's force in the north and Nogi's 3rd Army had each suffered over 20,000 casualties in the month of August.

Consequently, Kuropatkin's army outnumbered Oyama's by 33 per cent when he conducted his own offensive on 22 September along the Sha-Ho River on a nearly 60km front. Oyama's men held their ground in the face of attacks that resulted in approximately 40,000 Russian and about half as many Japanese casualties. At the end of this two-week battle, both sides remained in place, settling into defensive positions in which they intended to spend the winter. These positions overlooked an increasingly bleak no-man's land. This would serve as the battlefield for a further climactic pitched battle the following February – Mukden.

During November and December, there was little major activity on either side along the Sha-Ho River. The Russians dug extensive defensive positions and shelters while the Japanese constructed somewhat less elaborate positions, not intending to fight another defensive battle. Both Kuropatkin's and Oyama's armies attempted to pull forward replacements, trying to bring their battalions up to strength after the brutal battles.

Throughout the winter, Kuropatkin continuously delayed any offensive action, hoping to wait until he could achieve overwhelming numerical superiority sometime in early 1905. Oyama also delayed, both to consolidate and reorganize his armies, and in the expectation of imminent victory for Nogi at Port Arthur. On 2 January 1905, his waiting paid off when Gen Anatoly Stoessel signed a surrender document with Nogi and marched more than 40,000 Russian troops into captivity.

MISHCHENKO'S CAVALRY RAID

After the surrender of Port Arthur, the Japanese high command recognized a narrow window of opportunity to quickly mass and defeat the remaining Russian armies at Mukden. Having successfully captured Port Arthur,

Nogi's 3rd Army was theoretically available to join the main force for a final offensive against Kuropatkin. However, 3rd Army's availability was only theoretical for the time being, as in the course of nine months it had suffered nearly 60,000 casualties out of an establishment strength of 100,000 at its peak. Additionally, the tasks of accepting the surrender of nearly 40,000 Russian prisoners, interning them, occupying Port Arthur itself, receiving replacements and re-equipping the army for future operations were considerable. Despite these factors, the Japanese could still achieve a favourable ratio of forces in the next battle if Nogi could quickly consolidate and reorganize his forces, then rapidly march them nearly 300km north to join Oyama.

A Russian battalion on the march near San-de-pu. They wear the M1881 greatcoat and black manchzhurka – fur hat – ubiquitous among Russians at Mukden. (Maidun Collection/Alamy Stock Photo)

Speed would be key, as this window of opportunity was evident to the Russians as well. While Kuropatkin and his commanders preferred to delay and wait for as many reinforcements as possible, they recognized the advantage gained by launching an attack before Nogi joined Oyama.

Both Japanese and Russian generals considered these factors between 2 and 25 January, when the 2nd Manchurian Army initiated the battle of San-de-pu. However, in the intervening three weeks, the Russians conducted the largest and most significant cavalry operation of the war. In an effort to disrupt Japanese concentrations south of Mukden, Kuropatkin dispatched General of Cavalry Pavel Mishchenko with approximately 7,500 cavalrymen, divided into three 'columns': the western, centre and eastern.

The Russians had considered conducting a deep cavalry raid to disrupt the Japanese lines of supply for several months. The Russian staff envisioned this to coincide with a general offensive by the whole Russian army across the Japanese front along the Sha-Ho. After the fall of Port Arthur, Major General (Maj Gen) Aleksei Evert, the Russian quartermaster general, recommended that the time was ripe to conduct a deep, large-scale cavalry raid. In his view, such a raid would be useful if conducted immediately as an independent action, as it would disrupt the redeployment of Nogi's army. This would allow Kuropatkin to prepare for and initiate his own offensive before the Japanese had massed their forces.

Despite high expectations, Mishchenko's cavalry raid accomplished little, and may have even expedited Nogi's march to the north. (Author's collection)

Mishchenko began his mission on the morning of 9 January, heading west by south-west from a starting point behind the Russian right (western) flank on the Sha-Ho line. His primary task was to destroy the Japanese supply depot at Newchuang (also called Yinkou), about 100km to the south-west of the Japanese main army's left (western) flank. A second priority of Mishchenko's raid was to

cut the Japanese rail line to Port Arthur, further east of Newchuang, which could only be effectively accomplished if several important rail bridges were destroyed.

During the eight-day operation, the Russian cavalry did not live up to high expectations. Throughout the operation, Mishchenko's force averaged a pace of approximately 21 miles a day, hardly faster than motivated infantry. Moreover, the Russian subordinate commands displayed little initiative and consistently overestimated the strength of Japanese units they encountered. On 12 January, perhaps the decisive day of the operation, Mishchenko made a detailed but overly cautious plan of attack on Newchuang. Mishchenko dedicated only 15 squadrons for the attack, with his remaining 56 squadrons fulfilling supporting or security tasks. After delaying the attack to the afternoon, Mishchenko eventually committed just 1,100 or so men to the attack on the actual depot, which was manned by 400 Japanese infantry. This ratio grew more unfavourable for the Russians when, at 1630hrs, a Japanese train suddenly pulled into Newchuang, bringing 700 more Japanese infantry into the fortified depot. This all unfolded in view of five squadrons of Russian cavalry, who fired at the train as it approached and entered the Japanese lines.

When the Russian attack on Newchuang finally began, it was not properly supported or coordinated. During the attack itself, Mishchenko began to worry about Japanese forces cutting off his line of retreat. Instead of the assault on Newchuang, he focused his attention on the operations isolating the objective, and suddenly began to withdraw from the Newchuang area before the depot had been seized. After a few spirited attempts, Colonel (Col) Khoranov, the officer in charge of the actual assault, called off the attack after having suffered 300 casualties. Mishchenko's force rapidly returned north over the next three days, avoiding several attempts by Japanese cavalry and infantry units to cut them off by seizing river crossings and other passes.

During the whole operation from 9–16 January, Mishchenko suffered 400 casualties, or just more than 5 per cent of his force. While these losses were not inconsequential, they seem inordinately light, given the duration, significance and potential upside of pressing the attack at this stage of the war, suggesting a lack of resolve or overabundance of caution. The Russians' only tangible achievements were cutting several telegraph and telephone lines and destroying two trains. Otherwise, the effect of the operation on disrupting Japanese plans was negligible, as the Japanese responded by shifting only a modest number of second-echelon units.

The original goal of the raid as recommended by Evert was to disrupt or delay the concentration of the Japanese armies. In this context, it was a total failure. It may have even expedited the concentration of the Japanese armies, as Oyama's headquarters quickly issued march orders to nearly all of Nogi's units when the scale of the raid was discovered on 13 January. The 1st,

Though the cavalry was increasingly fighting dismounted or performing reconnaissance duties, there were some instances of mounted combat and charges at San-de-pu and Mukden. (Photo by Fine Art Images/Heritage Images/Getty Images)

7th and 9th Divisions, as well as two additional Kobi (reserve) brigades, received orders to begin their march north to occupy the left wing of the Japanese force. Nogi marched the men rather than attempting to transport them by train or otherwise, believing that the exercise would be good to ready the troops for a battle of manoeuvre after the siege of Port Arthur. Nogi's remaining division from the period of the siege, the veteran 11th Division, was ordered to link up with the 1st Kobi Division. The resulting force would be reflagged as the 5th Japanese Army, or Yalu Army, and would be commanded by Gen Kawamura. This organizational change would prove pivotal to the Japanese plans for the battle of Mukden.

THE BATTLE OF SAN-DE-PU

After the failure of Mishchenko's cavalry raid, it was inevitable that Nogi's army would soon join Oyama. This prompted Kuropatkin on 19 January to issue the orders for his long-awaited offensive. The Russian armies would attack en echelon from west to east, with Grippenberg's 2nd Manchurian Army as the main effort. Grippenberg would attack the extreme left of the Japanese armies, seizing a 20km-wide portion of the Japanese front centred on the villages of San-de-pu and Hei-kou-tai. Kuropatkin's plan presumed that this would cause the Japanese positions on the left to collapse and lead to a general retreat of the Japanese 2nd Army south towards Liaoyang. Kuropatkin gave instructions to Linevich and Kaulbars to attack in support of Grippenberg as his offensive developed and expanded. This was an altogether conservative plan, as the execution of each subsequent unit's attack was contingent on the success of the previous.

The Russian forces under Kuropatkin consisted of approximately 300,000 combatants, including nearly 50,000 directly under Kuropatkin as a general reserve. However, the battle as it actually transpired would only involve Grippenberg's army, consisting of four corps (VIII and X Corps, 1st Siberian and the Rifle Corps), in all some 96,000 infantry and 9,000 cavalry.

The Japanese armies, still awaiting the arrival of Nogi's 3rd Army, probably comprised only 180,000 troops in January 1905. The Japanese disposition on the left flank compounded this disparity. The Japanese lines were relatively undermanned along the 20km of front where Grippenberg would attack. In total, the Japanese forces located on Grippenberg's multi-village objective consisted of only 18 squadrons of cavalry, four battalions of infantry, a few engineer companies, several machine guns and six cannons. While the Japanese 2nd Army did have its own dedicated reserve – the 3rd Division – the Japanese defences would ultimately rest on Oyama's ability to leverage his general reserve, consisting of the 5th Division, 8th Division and 8th Kobi Brigade (maybe 30,000 troops in all). These forces were located 20km

A battery of eight 76.2mm M1900 field guns bombard the Japanese lines. (Photo by DeAgostini/Getty Images)

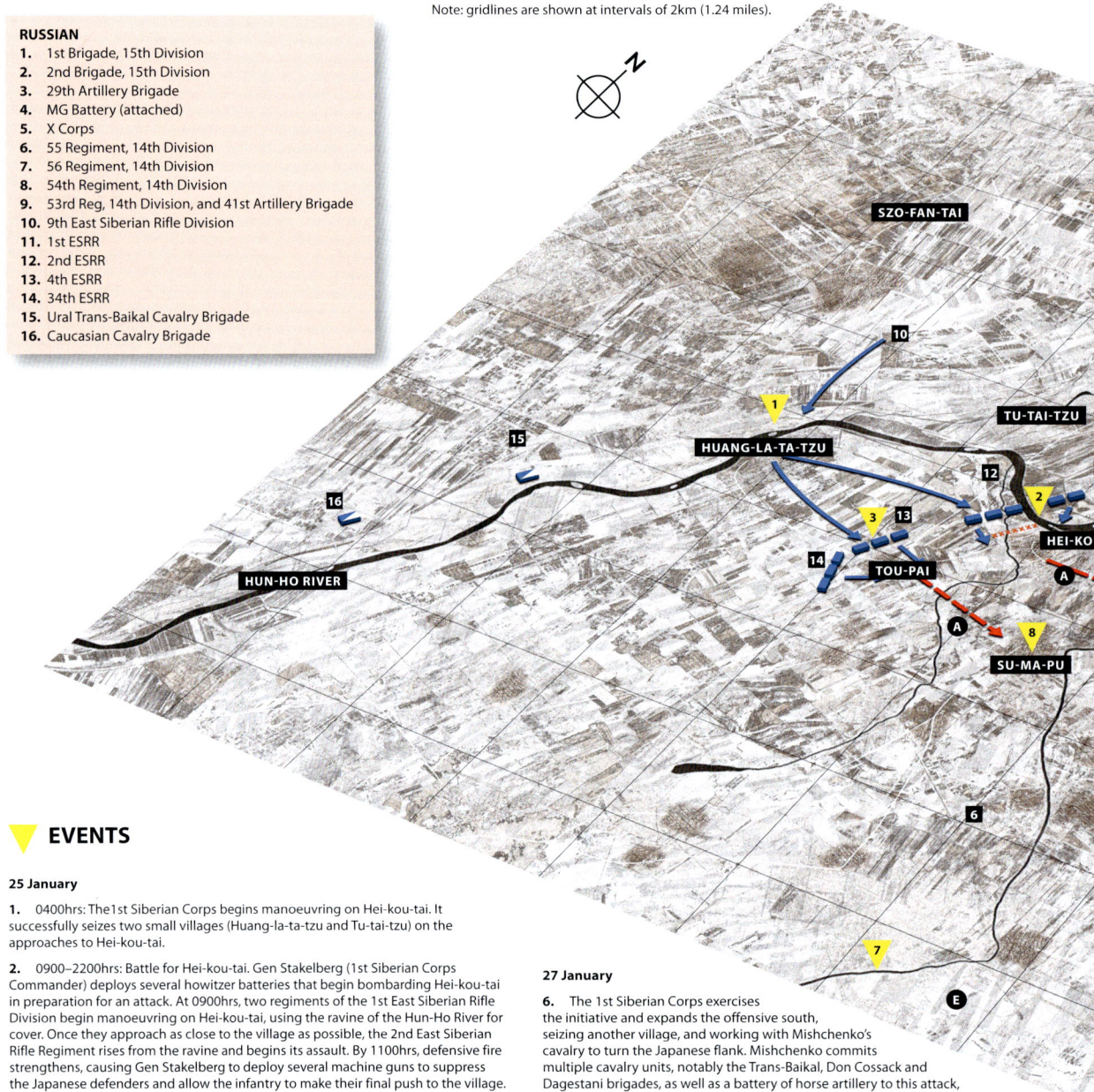

RUSSIAN
1. 1st Brigade, 15th Division
2. 2nd Brigade, 15th Division
3. 29th Artillery Brigade
4. MG Battery (attached)
5. X Corps
6. 55 Regiment, 14th Division
7. 56 Regiment, 14th Division
8. 54th Regiment, 14th Division
9. 53rd Reg, 14th Division, and 41st Artillery Brigade
10. 9th East Siberian Rifle Division
11. 1st ESRR
12. 2nd ESRR
13. 4th ESRR
14. 34th ESRR
15. Ural Trans-Baikal Cavalry Brigade
16. Caucasian Cavalry Brigade

▼ EVENTS

25 January

1. 0400hrs: The 1st Siberian Corps begins manoeuvring on Hei-kou-tai. It successfully seizes two small villages (Huang-la-ta-tzu and Tu-tai-tzu) on the approaches to Hei-kou-tai.

2. 0900–2200hrs: Battle for Hei-kou-tai. Gen Stakelberg (1st Siberian Corps Commander) deploys several howitzer batteries that begin bombarding Hei-kou-tai in preparation for an attack. At 0900hrs, two regiments of the 1st East Siberian Rifle Division begin manoeuvring on Hei-kou-tai, using the ravine of the Hun-Ho River for cover. Once they approach as close to the village as possible, the 2nd East Siberian Rifle Regiment rises from the ravine and begins its assault. By 1100hrs, defensive fire strengthens, causing Gen Stakelberg to deploy several machine guns to suppress the Japanese defenders and allow the infantry to make their final push to the village. By 2200hrs the 2nd East Siberian Rifles enters Hei-kou-tai. Once the Siberians gain a foothold in the Japanese fortifications, they quickly kill the Japanese defenders and seize the rest of the partially burning village. 1st Siberian Corps' seizure of Hei-kou-tai is Grippenburg's precondition for VIII Corps' attack on San-de-pu.

3. The 35th ESRR attacks and seizes the village of Tou-pai to the south of Hei-kou-tei, solidifying 1st Siberian Corps' position.

4. Oyama acts decisively in response to the Russian attack. He immediately reinforces the Japanese left flank with one Kobi brigade (roughly 5,000 soldiers) directly into the village of San-de-pu, plus the entire 8th Division to reinforce the Japanese 2nd Army (Oku) as a whole. San-de-pu is not attacked, as Grippenburg directs VIII Corps to wait until Hei-kou-tai is seized.

26 January

5. Grippenberg initiates VIII Corps assault on San-de-pu, with 1st Siberian Corps in support (from Hei-kou-tai). The VIII Corps launches the 14th Division against San-de-pu, but a fierce snowstorm limits visibility and causes confusion for all manoeuvring forces that day. 15th Division assaults the wrong village, a mistake resulting from the heavy snowfall and limited visibility. The VIII Corps assault on San-de-pu is unsuccessful. Meanwhile the Japanese launch their own attack against the 1st Siberian Corps units at Hei-kou-tai resulting in fierce close quarter fighting throughout the day. 1st Siberian Corps successfully defends Hei-kou-tai.

27 January

6. The 1st Siberian Corps exercises the initiative and expands the offensive south, seizing another village, and working with Mishchenko's cavalry to turn the Japanese flank. Mishchenko commits multiple cavalry units, notably the Trans-Baikal, Don Cossack and Dagestani brigades, as well as a battery of horse artillery to this attack, aimed at enveloping the Japanese left (western) flank. At one point on the 27th, Stackelberg and Mishchenko's offensive actions began to bend the Japanese left flank back on itself.

7. The Japanese 5th Infantry Division (the last of Oyama's general reserve) and a cavalry brigade are able to stop Mishchenko's attack.

8. 2130hrs: The 1st Siberian Corps makes one last mass assault on Su-ma-pu in an attempt to turn the San-de-pu position. It is unsuccessful. The assault consists of 12 battalions of infantry in two dense columns in a night bayonet attack. The columns make it to within 600 yards of the village without detection, at which point a storm of rifle and machine-gun fire open up and destroy the attacking columns. Two of the assaulting battalions, those of the 6th Rifle Regiment, lose 21 of 23 officers and 1,150 out of 1,500 soldiers killed, wounded or missing in the attack.

29 January

9. Japanese launch counter-attack. The 5th and 8th Divisions ferociously attack the Russian units around San-de-pu and in Hei-kou-tai. Meanwhile, Oku orders a bombardment of the Russian lines east of San-de-pu, which causes Kuropatkin to fear that the Japanese may open another offensive along the seam of the attacking 2nd Manchurian Army and currently passive 3rd Manchurian Army. These actions cause Kuropatkin to call off the Russian offensive and order a retreat north of the Hun-Ho River. 1st Siberian Corps is forced to abandon Hei-kou-tai after five days of combat.

THE BATTLE OF SAN-DE-PU, 25–29 JANUARY 190

On 25 February, Kuropatkin launches Grippenberg's 2nd Manchurian Army in an assault on Oku's 2nd Japanese Army's position around the villages of San-de-pu and Hei-kou-tai. The fighting is very bloody, and takes place during a brutal snowstorm. Despite heavy losses on both sides, Kuropatkin calls off the offensive on the 29th, giving back the meager gains of the Russians. This map shows the dispositions and actions on 25 January and includes a description of the course of the full battle.

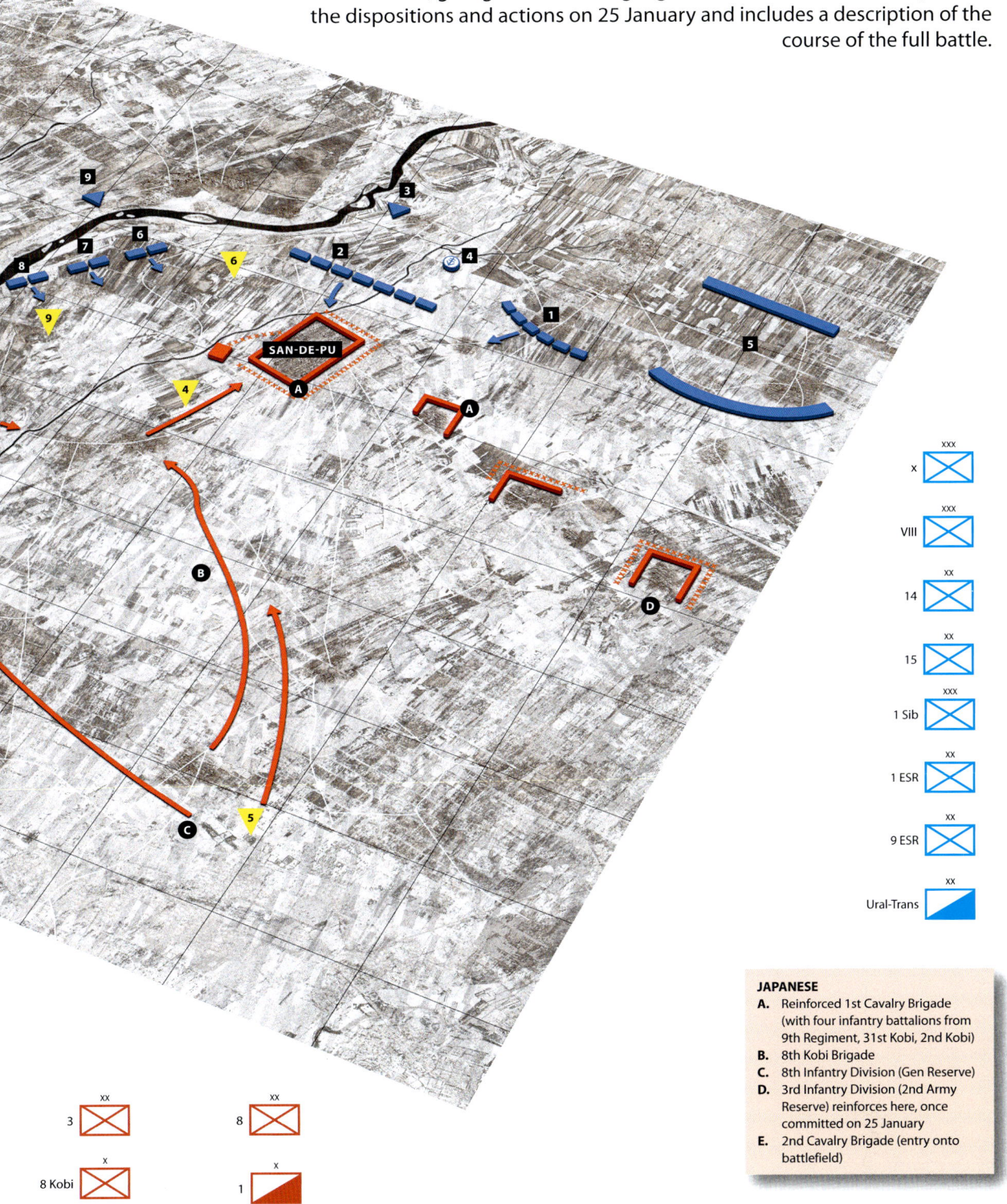

JAPANESE
- **A.** Reinforced 1st Cavalry Brigade (with four infantry battalions from 9th Regiment, 31st Kobi, 2nd Kobi)
- **B.** 8th Kobi Brigade
- **C.** 8th Infantry Division (Gen Reserve)
- **D.** 3rd Infantry Division (2nd Army Reserve) reinforces here, once committed on 25 January
- **E.** 2nd Cavalry Brigade (entry onto battlefield)

Japanese 8th Division staff, part of Oku's 2nd Army, observing the enemy lines near Hei-kou-tai. (Author's collection)

or more away, and would require an adept commander to quickly identify the decisive point of the action and commit the appropriate forces in time. In total, the Japanese had 41 battalions, five squadrons, 108 guns and several machine guns within 24km of the front at San-de-pu – giving the Russians approximately a 20:1 advantage at the outset of the battle, and still a 2:1 advantage when considering the entire area of the operation.

Japanese defensive preparations on the front lines partially compensated for inferior numbers. The villages Grippenberg sought to capture, initially Hei-kou-tai and San-de-pu, were fortified and therefore served as ready-made redoubts. Furthermore, both armies were better integrating machine guns at this point in the war, with the Japanese achieving a higher density of as many as two machine guns per battalion in some divisions. Oyama had just completed a push to deliver more machine guns to the front-line troops below Mukden. These machine guns would be especially effective in the battle of San-de-pu, where fortified villages were the focal points of assaults involving several battalions over open terrain.

Adding to the difficulty and misery of the Russian attackers in the coming battle was the cold weather during the period 25–29 January. Temperatures would drop below zero degrees Fahrenheit at night, and would not break above freezing during the day. Additionally, a strong wind swept across the open landscape during the battle, occasionally blowing in a heavy snowfall. Wounded soldiers would face hypothermia and death if they could not crawl, walk or be carried back to the rear within a few hours. Attacking soldiers who did not seize their objectives fared especially poorly in this context, as they generally lacked cover and concealment from which friendly troops could drag or carry them back to the rear.

On the first day of the Battle of San-de-pu, the 1st Siberian Corps successfully seized Hei-kou-tai, but only after fighting from 0900hrs to 2200hrs. This fatally delayed the VIII Corps attack on San-de-pu, which was planned to begin only after Hei-kou-tai was in Russian hands. On the 26th, the VIII Corps attacked San-de-pu during blizzard-like conditions, and failed to seize their objective. Oyama proved extremely decisive in reinforcing his 2nd Army from the first day of the attack, eventually sending all of his reserves to halt Grippenburg's 2nd Manchurian Army. Meanwhile, Kuropatkin's other armies, 2nd and 3rd Manchurian, remained inactive to the east of the battle. Fighting continued on the 27th and 28th, with no decisive developments. By the 29 January, Oyama ordered Oku to counter-attack the 2nd Manchurian Army, and to bombard part of Kaulbar's 3rd Manchurian Army in the centre.

Villages such as these dotted the landscape around Mukden, providing excellent cornerstones to defensive lines. (Author's collection)

This caused Kuropatkin to fear a general Japanese counter-attack along his whole front. Electing to make defensive preparations, Kuropatkin ordered Grippenburg to call off the attack, and return to his starting position. (For more detail on the Battle of San-de-pu, see pp.16–17)

The failure of San-de-pu must be placed primarily on Kuropatkin's unwillingness or inability to support the 2nd Manchurian Army with his other two armies – that is, expand the army-level attack into a general offensive along the whole front. The lack of pressure on the Japanese along the lines of the 1st and 3rd Manchurian Armies allowed Oyama to commit all of his reserves to stopping Grippenberg's offensive, and then to aggressively counter-attack. Furthermore, Kuropatkin failed to force any dilemmas onto Oyama, while the mere suggestion of a Japanese counter-stroke in the east caused him to call off his offensive altogether and return to the defensive. This all transpired in the context of Russian numerical superiority, which exceeded the Japanese by as much as 50 per cent in this part of the battlefield. One positive explanation for Kuropatkin's decisions, though this can only be deduced from actual actions taken, is that he was not actually committed to offensive operation at this stage of the war, merely hoping to disrupt the Japanese until further reinforcements could arrive.

The rank and file suffered heavy losses despite Kuropatkin's caution. In four days of combat, 11,000 Russians and perhaps 9,000 Japanese were casualties along an active front of about 12km. Most of these casualties were centred on Hei-kou-tai and San-de-pu, and the 1st Siberian Corps bore the brunt of losses for the Russians. From 25–28 January, it lost 7,000 men out of its total strength of 19,000.

Further demoralizing the Russian rank and file was the 'desertion' of Gen Grippenberg. Grippenberg telegraphed St Petersburg on 30 January, at first requesting to be recalled due to ill-health. Upon prompting by the army staff in St Petersburg, he admitted that the real reason for his request was his inability to exercise independent command with Kuropatkin as his superior. Without discussing the issue with Kuropatkin, Tsar Nicholas II approved Grippenberg's request, which in Kuropatkin's opinion severely undermined morale and discipline in the Manchurian armies. This unexpected loss caused Kuropatkin to shuffle army commanders during a decisive point in the war. He placed Kaulbars in command of what had been Grippenberg's 2nd Manchurian Army and gave a corps commander, Bilderling, command of Kaulbars' 3rd Manchurian Army. Linevich remained in command of the 1st Manchurian Army on the Russian left flank.

The 106mm M1877 '42 line gun' siege gun. The 3rd Manchurian Army had 20 such pieces in the centre of the battlefield. (Chronicle/Alamy Stock Photo)

Grippenberg observing a retreating field gun. He would successfully petition to be recalled to St Petersburg after the battle. (Paul Thiriat, 'La retraite de Sandepon' [1905] from the Anne S.K. Brown Military Collection, Brown Digital Repository, Brown University Library)

CHRONOLOGY

1904

8/9 February	Japanese attack on Russian Pacific Squadron at Port Arthur.
30 April–1 May	Kuroki defeats Zasulich in the first battle of the war on the Yalu River.
5 May	Oku's 2nd Army lands on the Liaodong Peninsula.
14–15 June	Battle of Telissu. Decisive Japanese victory that ends attempted Russian relief of Port Arthur.
10 July	Battle of Motien Pass. Kuroki forces his way through the mountains on the way to Liaoyang.
7 August	Gen Nogi's 3rd Army begins its assault on Port Arthur.
26 August–3 September	Battle of Liaoyang. Kuropatkin retreats to defensive line along the Sha-Ho River.
11–17 October	Russian counter-offensive along the Sha-Ho is bloody but inconclusive.

1905

2 January	Port Arthur surrenders.
9–16 January	Mishchenko's cavalry raid on Yinkou/Newchuang.
13 January	Oyama's headquarters issues orders to Nogi to begin movement north to join the armies south of Mukden.
22 January	In St Petersburg, Russian troops fire on crowd – remembered as 'Bloody Sunday'. The Revolution of 1905 begins.
25–29 January	Kuropatkin's 2nd Manchurian Army under Grippenberg attacks Oku's 2nd Army at the battle of San-de-pu.
19 February	Kawamura's 5th (Yalu) Army begins movement towards Chenghocheng – beginning the battle of Mukden.
22 February	Gen Alexeiv launches a counter-attack against Kawamura's force – it is unsuccessful.
23–24 February	Kawamura's Yalu Army fights a vicious battle for a series of hills around the village of Chenghocheng, defeating Alexeiv's detachment. Kuropatkin orders Rennenkampf to take over the detachment.
25 February	Kuroki's 1st Army begins attacking Linevich's 1st Manchurian Army in attempt to turn the east flank of his 3rd Siberian Corps.
26 February	Rennenkampf takes command of the Chenghocheng Detachment and orders a retreat to Fountain Hill.

27 February	Redoubt 16 stormed. General bombardment in the centre of the battlefield. Nogi initiates his advance in the west.
28 February	Kuropatkin begins forming a 'western screen' to halt Nogi's advance.
1 March	Heavy fighting begins west of Mukden, and spreads across the entire front, nearly 90 miles.
3 March	Kuropatkin moves his headquarters to Mukden and determines to counter-attack on the 4th or 5th.
4 March	Oyama commits his last reserve, three Kobi brigades, to strengthen Nogi's envelopment.
5 March	Kaulbars conducts a counter-attack west of Mukden.
6 March	Kuropatkin puts together a second, larger counter-attack including Gerngross' 1st Siberian Corps veterans. It is unable to halt Nogi's continuing envelopment.
7 March	Kuropatkin orders 1st and 2nd Manchurian Armies to retreat to the Hun-Ho River defensive line during the night of 7/8 March.
8 March	Rennenkampf, Linevich and Bilderling's forces successfully retreat to the Hun-Ho River.
9 March	Kuropatkin orders Muilov to counter-attack, assaulting the northern flank of Nogi's wheel. By this point, Nogi has extended his line, resulting in heavy, inconclusive fighting. The Russian position continues to deteriorate. Kuropatkin issues orders for a retreat on the 10th.
10 March	Early morning – Japanese attacks against Russian forces west of Mukden. Noon – Japanese Guards Division advances north-west towards Nogi's position. Kuropatkin has an 8-mile, closing gap through which to extricate his army. 1600hrs – Kuropatkin's army escapes to the north, except for numerous rearguard elements. 1600hrs–1900hrs – Kuropatkin's remaining security elements collapse as Japanese divisions break in all around Mukden. Ganenfeldt's force is annihilated.
11–13 March	Kuropatkin's forces retreat to Tieh-ling and establish a line on the Fan-Ho River.
14 March	Kuroki's 2nd Division attacks Zasulich's force on the Fan-Ho River.
14–24 March	Russian forces retreat to Hsi-ping-kai.
16 March	Kuropatkin is relieved. Linevich takes command of the Russian armies.
April–August	The Japanese occupy positions north of Tieh-ling, facing the Russians south of Hsi-ping-kai. Both sides build strength and conduct numerous cavalry raids for the remaining months of the war.
6–30 August	Russian and Japanese delegations meet at Portsmouth, New Hampshire, where US President Theodore Roosevelt acts as moderator.
5 September	Peace is signed at Portsmouth. The Russo-Japanese War is over.

OPPOSING COMMANDERS

RUSSIAN

Nearly all of the senior Russian commanders had decades of command, staff, and combat experience. However, by 1905, their experience in the Russo-Turkish War was a faded memory, and the experience of fighting in Central Asia and the Boxer Rebellion was insufficient to prepare these commanders for the war in Manchuria. The fighting from May 1904 until January 1905 was a brutal instructor to these commanders, and all the officers and men in their armies were forced to adapt to survive.

In February 1904, *The Times*' military correspondent wrote of **General of Infantry Aleksey Nikolaevich Kuropatkin (1848–1912)**: 'The General stands higher than any other Russian officer, not only in Russian opinion, but in that of professional soldiers all the world over, and if any human agency can change the deplorable situation to Russia's advantage, Kuropatkin may be the man to do it.'[6] While he would ultimately fail to meet the enormous expectations placed upon him, Kuropatkin's lack of success in Manchuria was not due to a lack of intelligence, experience or competence. On the contrary, he possessed all of these qualities, and in February 1904 he seemed to be the best military officer in Russia to take command in Manchuria.

Born into a military family in 1848, Kuropatkin graduated from the Pavlovsk War School at the age of 18 and entered service in the army as a lieutenant in the 1st Turkestan Rifle Battalion in 1866. He would serve in Central Asia for ten years, culminating in a campaign as a staff officer for the famous Gen Mikhail Skobelev's campaign in the Khanate of Kokand (roughly modern-day Uzbekistan) in 1876.

Kuropatkin gained further experience on Skobelev's staff in the Russo-Turkish War of 1877–78. Kuropatkin's rise continued post-1878 when he served in yet another Central Asian campaign in 1880–81. In 1890, he was promoted to lieutenant general, and in 1898, the tsar would appoint him as his Minister of War. While he opposed the imperial and commercial interests that led Russia into war with Japan, Kuropatkin was nevertheless appointed commander of the Russian Army in Manchuria in February, and later supreme commander of Russian forces in East Asia in October 1904.

Kuropatkin commanded the Russian Army in a period of extremely rapid societal and technological changes. He would reach the apogee of his career

---

6   Aleksei Kuropatkin, *Russian Army and the Japanese War*, trans. Capt. A. B. Linsday (London: 1909), v. Taken from Translator's Preface.

commanding armies of hundreds of thousands of soldiers spread out over dozens of kilometres. He would leverage the telegraph, field telephone and even an automobile to communicate with his subordinates. These developments in warfare would prove taxing to all armies and commanders in the coming decades. Notwithstanding these challenges, Kuropatkin's deficiencies as a commander seem in retrospect to have been those that have always derailed commanders. While it can be argued that he was frequently overly cautious, at Mukden, Kuropatkin was simply less cunning, less wilful and less confident in driving the pace of events, and incapable of correctly assessing his enemy's course of action.

Kuropatkin was as prepared as any general officer for high command, but during the Mukden campaign he failed to discern his opponents' scheme of manoeuvre. (Photo by Universal History Archive/Universal Images Group via Getty Images)

General Nikolai Petrovich Linevich (1838–1908) commanded the 1st Manchurian Army at the battle of Mukden. Linevich joined the army in 1855 (during the Crimean War), and also served in the Russo-Turkish War (1877–78). He was the commander of international coalition forces for the relief of Peking during the Boxer Relief Expedition of 1900 and would lead the victory parade in Peking on 28 August that year. While he was awarded the Order of St George for his accomplishments in China, Sergei Witte later noted with dismay: 'One Lieutenant General [almost certainly Linevich] … returned to his post in the Amur region with ten trunks full of valuables coming from the looted Peking palaces.'[7] After the Boxer Rebellion, Linevich remained in the east, serving as commander-in-chief of the Priamur region from 1903 until the outbreak of war in 1904. At the beginning of the war, he commanded the 1st Manchurian Army until the arrival of Kuropatkin in March 1904.

In November 1904, Linevich would again take command of the 1st Manchurian Army, due to Russian reinforcements necessitating the creation of further Manchurian armies. Linevich was 67 years old at the time of Mukden, ten years older than his superior, Kuropatkin. He was competent enough in defence, and proved capable in assessing opportunities for counter-attacks, but lacked either the initiative or skill as a subordinate to influence Kuropatkin to capitalize on these opportunities. While not outstanding at Mukden, the tsar appointed Linevich overall commander in Manchuria after Kuropatkin stepped down in March 1905. Linevich would remain in command through to the end of the war and during the period of mutinies in Manchuria from 1905–06.

One American observer of the war met Linevich after Mukden. Though he noted that Linevich was missing most of his top teeth, the American described him in mostly positive terms. (Photo by Rischgitz/Getty Images)

General Aleksandr Vasilievich Kaulbars (1844–1929) commanded the Russian 2nd Manchurian Army at the battle of Mukden. Born into a Protestant family of Baltic–German ancestry (a proportionately overrepresented demographic among Russian generals), he joined the army at a young age and spent much of his early career in Central Asia. Like his peers, Kaulbars also served in the

---

7   Diana Preston, *The Boxer Rebellion* (New York: Walker and Company, 1999), 302.

Gen Rennenkampf would finish the war with an enhanced reputation, rising to command the Russian 1st Army in 1914. (The Picture Art Collection/ Alamy Stock Photo)

Russo-Turkish War and was eventually assigned to aid and advise the new Bulgarian Army. He served for one year as War Minister for Bulgaria in 1882. In October 1904, Kuropatkin pulled Kaulbars to Manchuria to serve as the commander of the new 3rd Manchurian Army. After the battle of San-de-pu in January 1905, Kuropatkin gave Kaulbars command of the 2nd Manchurian Army after Grippenberg's departure.

Aleksandr Aleksandrovich Bilderling (1846–1912) commanded the Russian 3rd Manchurian Army at the battle of Mukden. In Manchuria, he took command of XVII Corps – a Regular Army (European) Corps that arrived in Manchuria in May 1904. He commanded the corps in many battles during the summer and autumn, including Liaoyang and the Sha-Ho. After Grippenberg's resignation and Kaulbars' advancement, Bilderling was promoted to army command and given the 3rd Manchurian Army. He was relieved following the battle of Mukden, resuming command of his old corps for the remainder of the war.

Pavel (Paul) Karlovich von Rennenkampf (1854–1918) commanded the Chenghocheng Detachment, a mixed cavalry–infantry formation on the Russian left flank during the battle of Mukden. Like Kaulbars, Rennenkampf was born into a noble, Baltic–German family in Russia in 1854. By the time he was 17, he had graduated from a military school in Helsinki and was commissioned into the cavalry. He later completed the General Staff School and, in 1882, joined the Russian General Staff. In 1895, he commanded a cavalry regiment, serving with some distinction in the occupation of Manchuria during the Boxer Rebellion.

Rennenkampf began the war as the commander of the Trans-Baikal Cavalry Division and would be one of the few outstanding Russian general officers in the war. He fought in several early battles until wounded in the thigh after the battle of Motien Pass. After recovering from his wounds, he returned to duty, fighting at Liaoyang and the Sha-Ho. His subordinates spoke highly of him as a commander. At Mukden, Kuropatkin positioned Rennenkampf on the Russian left flank, where his formation held its ground in the face of furious assaults from the Japanese 5th (Yalu) Army. Unfortunately, the outcome of the battle would be decided on the opposite flank of the army. After the war, Rennenkampf commanded troops to put down mutinous soldiers during the 1905 Russian Revolution. Rennenkampf would eventually rise to command the Russian 1st Army in the Tannenberg campaign of August 1914.

JAPANESE

The Japanese commanders were soldiers of the Meiji period. They benefited from the decision of the Meiji government to embrace the benefits of westernization and most were sent overseas to receive professional military education, primarily in France and Germany.

Field Marshal Iwao Oyama (1842–1916) served as the commander-in-chief of all Japanese land forces in Manchuria during the war. With the exception of Port Arthur, Oyama served as field commander in all the major battles of the war: Lioayang, the Sha-Ho, San-de-pu and Mukden.

Oyama was born in the Satusma province in 1842 into a samurai family and would fight against the Shogun's forces in the Boshin War. Later, after joining the Imperial Japanese Army, he travelled and studied in France, and was an observer during the Franco-Prussian War in 1870. He returned to Japan and commanded imperial conscripts during the Satsuma Rebellion of 1877. Oyama rose to serve as Deputy Army Minister and Deputy Navy Minister before the First Sino-Japanese War (1894–95). He distinguished himself while commanding the 2nd Army when it besieged and then seized Lüshunkou (Port Arthur).

By February 1905, Oyama was confident after his string of successful battles in the war. He believed and intended that the coming battle at Mukden would be decisive. He set his five armies into motion in February 1904 with the intention of reproducing the 1870 Prussian victory at Sedan, but on an even grander scale.

As a young man, **General Tametomo Kuroki (1844–1923)** fought in the Boshin War, and for the Japanese Emperor in the Satsuma Rebellion. He was promoted to command the 6th Division in the Sino-Japanese War, resulting in his promotion to general and commander of the 1st Japanese Army by November 1903. When war began with Russia in February 1904, his army was the first deployed to Korea. From there, he experienced a series of successes from the Yalu, to Liaoyang and the Sha-Ho. He and his army were both experienced and reliable.

British journalist Frederick Palmer observed Gen Kuroki's 1st Japanese Army from its landing in Korea until the battle of Liaoyang. Reflecting on his experiences in November 1904, Palmer wrote: 'General Kuroki spent most of his time in the shade. If his people (ever) raise a statue to him, I hope that he will not be riding a prancing horse and swinging his sword; for he never rode a prancing horse and never used his sword. To my recollection, I never saw him make any gesture except to salute. The sculptor had best make him squatting and looking at a map while he listens to his staff.'[8]

General Yasukata Oku (1846–1930) would command the Japanese 2nd Army and **General Michitsura Nodzu (1841–1907)** the Japanese 4th Army at Mukden. Both officers served with distinction during the Satsuma Rebellion of 1877, and afterwards both would study and observe abroad (Nodzu in the United States and Oku in Europe). In the 1880s, Nodzu commanded the Japanese 5th Division, which Oku would take

Oyama commanded forces larger than imaginable just a generation earlier. Nonetheless, he would never suffer defeat in the war. (Photo by Universal History Archive/Universal Images Group via Getty Images)

Despite his heroic pose, at least one contemporary observer described Kuroki as a practical officer, usually huddled over a map. (Syracuse University Art Museum/Bridgeman Images)

---

8 Frederick Palmer, *With Kuroki in Manchuria* (New York: Charles Scribner's Sons, 1904), 296.

Despite losing two sons at Port Arthur, Nogi would go on to fulfil his duty at Mukden a few months later. (Author's collection)

over and command during the Sino-Japanese War of 1894–95. Oku would eventually rise to army command in the war with China, taking over the Japanese 1st Army when its commander fell ill.

During the Russo-Japanese War, Oku's 2nd Army arrived early on, fighting in many of the initial battles, including Nanshan and Telissu. Later, when Nodzu's 4th Army also arrived in Manchuria, they would fight together with Kuroki's 1st Army under Oyama for the rest of the war. In these battles, Oyama tended to use Oku and Nodzu like an anvil, while Kuroki, and later Nogi or Kawamura, would serve as the hammer.

Like his peers, **General Kageaki Kawamura (1850–1926)** fought in the Boshin War, Satsuma Rebellion and Sino-Japanese War. Throughout 1904, Kawamura served successfully as commander of the 10th Division of Nodzu's 4th Army at Liaoyang and the Sha-Ho. In January 1905, he was selected over more senior officers for promotion to general and given command of the newly formed 5th (Yalu) Army. He was well rewarded for his performance at Mukden, and would be promoted to field marshal in 1915.

General Maresuke Nogi (1849–1912) commanded the Japanese 3rd Army during the battle of Mukden. Like his peers, Nogi had combat experience dating back to the Satsuma Rebellion, but was most famous for his service in the 1894–95 war with China. In 1894, he led the brigade that captured the Chinese port at Lüshunkou at the cost of only a few hundred casualties. For this reason, it is not surprising that he was recalled from retirement at the outbreak of war in 1904 and given command of the army that was tasked to seize the same port.

After arriving on the Liaodong Peninsula on 6 June 1904, Nogi wasted little time in seeking his own victory. In August, he ordered frontal attacks in the hope of a rapid success at Port Arthur, a method that earned him glory and fame a decade earlier as a brigade commander. Modern firepower and a well-led Russian defence would harshly rebuke his tactics, and Nogi was criticized during the siege of Port Arthur for being careless with the lives of Japanese soldiers. Nogi's two sons, both serving as officers in his army, were killed during the siege.

Despite the costliness of his tactics at Port Arthur, Nogi would eventually be vindicated when, on 2 January 1905, the Russian garrison capitulated. He was also able to efficiently re-equip and refit his army to participate in the Mukden campaign only six weeks later. His divisions were viewed as tempered veterans by other Japanese soldiers, and especially by Russian soldiers in the coming campaign. The battle of Mukden would be Nogi's first time operating in conjunction with other Japanese armies.

OPPOSING FORCES

RUSSIAN

The Imperial Russian Army had undergone significant restructuring and expansion since the reforms of Minister of War Dmitri Miliutin were initiated by Tsar Alexander II in 1874. Perhaps the most significant aspect of these reforms was the transition from a fully regular army to a reserve-based system – albeit with a still large regular army. By 1904, Russia had an active army of over a million soldiers, with as many as three times that number as reservists.

In contrast to Russia's last major war with Turkey in 1877–78, the war with Japan in 1904–05 would take place at the far reaches of the Eastern territories, thousands of miles from the centre of the empire. Russia would face an extremely aggressive and wilful army at the end of perhaps the longest land line of supply in history, the Trans-Siberian Railway system. It was under these conditions that Russia would activate its reserves and mobilize its post-reform army. During the war with Japan, and through the course of nine waves of mobilization, the Russian Army was able to summon 1,754,146 of these reservists and accept 1,174,913 of them into the ranks (some being rejected for age, illness or injury or receiving deferments). Once accepted into the army, the Ministry of War either used the reservists to bring regular units up to full strength, to stand up reserve units or to replace casualties incurred in Manchuria. By the war's end, half of the total troops in Manchuria were reservists.[9]

Russian officers expressed a profound preference for active service troops, frequently noting the reservists' higher propensity to complain, their lack of fitness and aggression, and their cynical view towards their service obligation. Officers such as Kuropatkin noted that the reservists seemed to have forgotten everything they had learned during their years of active service. The practical result of this was that officers tended to avoid appointing reservists for tasks that

Though the Russian infantry are in their summer uniform, this image portrays a standard formation when moving over open terrain. (From *A Photographic Record of the Russo-Japanese War*, P. F. Collier & Son, 1905)

---

9   Reese, *The Imperial Russian Army*, 194–197.

From November to January, Tsar Nicholas II's soldiers spent much of their time trying to stay warm and missing their distant homes. (Author's collection)

Both armies implemented existing structures, such as walls and enclosures, into their defensive systems. (The History Collection/Alamy Stock Photo)

required more initiative, such as outpost duty or patrolling. Despite the difficulties in incorporating mass numbers of reservists for the first time, the Russian soldiers continued to display remarkable resiliency in the face of repeated setbacks and retreats. The negative effects of the new reserve system seem to have been more notable on the home front than with units at the front. The activation and deployment of hundreds of thousands of reservists, many of whom were married with children, affected Russian families; they would previously have been more insulated from mobilization due to the nature of the old military system.

When the war began in February, there was no organized force in Manchuria above the level of brigade. It was not until August, six months after hostilities were initiated, that Russia finally massed a sizeable field army at the battle of Liaoyang. The army at Liaoyang reflected the difficulty of the mobilization efforts up to that point in the war, with only two of Kuropatkin's seven corps being from European Russia, while the remainder were corps from Siberian military districts. By February 1905, the number of 'European' corps, officially referred to as Army Corps, had increased to five, forming a substantial portion of the approximately 275,000 Russian 'bayonets' – or combat infantry – present for battle.[10]

By the battle of Mukden, many units in the Russian armies were veterans and had learned hard lessons over the past nine months of campaigning. This was especially true of the 1st and 3rd Siberian Corps, which had been in combat since the previous June. Units' experience of previous combat was evident in many ways, but especially in the increasing sophistication of defensive positions and field fortifications. Nine months earlier, at the battle of the Yalu in May 1904, the Russian artillery batteries were easily picked off as they were deployed in the open, on the summits or forward slopes of hills. By February 1905, Russian artillery batteries and machine guns were emplaced in planned dugouts, with sandbags or even brick walls solidifying the emplacement, and in many cases the positions were selected to avoid silhouetting themselves by elevation. Infantry positions were likewise generally well concealed and constructed to protect infantrymen from shrapnel. At the battalion level and higher, Russian defensive positions were complex, with multiple lines of trenches connecting to

10 Russian commanders at this time frequently referred to their actual and present combat troops as 'bayonets' for infantry, and 'sabres' for cavalry. This was done in an attempt to accurately communicate the combat value of a force rather than simply a count of all personnel in a formation.

fortified villages or hilltop redoubt systems. Units dug additional trench lines that extended out perpendicularly from the main line to provide a firing point into the 'dead space' in front of the trench line. In front of these positions, the Russians as a rule strung extensive barriers of single-strand wire (concertina wire was not yet fielded) in order to disrupt Japanese assaults.

Tactically, this was a difficult time for infantry assaults, and all armies organized along European lines were struggling to determine how to successfully conduct assaults without excessive losses. Fundamentally, armies were attempting to overcome the massive increase in firepower, which rifle and artillery improvements had created, without commensurate increases in mobility or protection. In essence, infantry units still attacked at the speeds and with the protection of early 19th-century regiments, but now faced massed bolt action rifles, machine guns and quick-firing smokeless artillery batteries. Furthermore, both sides in the Russo-Japanese War quickly improvised and employed grenades at scale, which added further dangers for the average rifleman.

Japanese infantry in early-war uniforms passing through wire obstacles. Though simple in concept and construction, these wire obstacles posed a terrible challenge to attacking infantry on both sides. (Photo by DeAgostini/Getty Images)

The Russian Army was mostly organized under standard European lines in 1904–05. The corps was the highest standing army formation, with armies being assembled from multiple corps as operations dictated. Up to December 1904, Kuropatkin organized the Russian ground forces into a single Manchurian Army. That December, the Manchurian Army had swollen to such a size that Kuropatkin split it first into two, then three separate field armies. Kuropatkin continued to serve as overall commander of this army group, which from that point forward consisted of the 1st, 2nd and 3rd Manchurian Armies.

Each of these armies generally consisted of three corps, designated either European or Siberian. These corps were standardized to contain

The 220th (Yepifan) Regiment of the 6th Siberian Corps. They are on the move somewhere in the centre of the Mukden battlefield, perhaps in the vicinity of Putilov Hill. (Sueddeutsche Zeitung Photo/Alamy Stock Photo)

approximately 41,000 troops in total,[11] including infantry, cavalry and artillery, but also engineer, sapper, telegraph, pontoon troops and more. At the time of the battle of Mukden, most of Kuropatkin's corps, and all the recently arrived European corps, fielded nearly their full complement of soldiers. However, the veterans of the 1st Siberian Army Corps only mustered 288 officers and some 12,000 soldiers due to casualties at San-de-pu. The main combat power of a corps were its two infantry divisions, one cavalry division and 102 cannon organized in batteries of either eight, or in the case of horse artillery, six guns.[12] Each infantry division typically consisted of two infantry brigades, which in turn comprised two infantry regiments. European regiments consisted of four battalions, while the Siberian regiments contained two or three, both generally made up of four companies. On campaign, a European regiment might contain approximately 3,100 soldiers in all, while the Siberian regiments were closer to 2,000.

The lowest standing echelon was the company, which on a war footing consisted of around 220 men. The company was broken down further into half-companies and platoons. When deployed defensively, a company might occupy a 400m front, and when in the attack, moved in two lines or waves. One Russian company commander, Captain L. Z. Soloviev, noted that by 1905, veterans were conducting attacks in a 'chain formation', in which soldiers moved individually with gaps of up to 10m between each soldier. In practice, this proved difficult at times, as the terrain frequently canalized troops towards certain low ground that protected them from fire but also bunched them together. At night, soldiers attacked much closer together, often shoulder-to-shoulder, as to do otherwise would court chaos and disorientation. This could still be effective, as it was difficult to effectively range and engage an enemy at night, even with direct fire.

Infantrymen were armed with the Three Line Rifle (signifying 7.62mm), Model 1891 Mosin-Nagant. This was a modern bolt action rifle that enabled units to engage enemies out to 2km. This is not to say individual soldiers could be effective at that range, for a number of reasons. Indeed, Russians frequently fired in volleys at the platoon level for reasons of control, both of the engagement itself and ammunition expenditure, and correct range finding. This allowed officers to achieve effective unit fire at longer ranges, by observing impacts and yelling out needed adjustments.

Since 1904, the Russians had purchased 'World Standard' Maxim machine guns, constructed on a carriage similar in concept to a field artillery gun. Russian forces grouped them into machine-gun companies of four to eight guns. These were a division-level asset in the formations that possessed them, though the Russians were overall deficient in this key weapon system. As an example, the 1st Manchurian Army – around 100,000 combatants – had only 22 machine guns in total. Interestingly, Kuropatkin sent a request to Moscow in the weeks leading up to Mukden for several hundred more machine guns of varying makes and manufacture, though only a fraction of these arrived before peace was made in September 1905. At Mukden, Kuropatkin's three armies had a total of only 56 machine guns.

The Russians did have an advantage in artillery at Mukden, though mostly in quantity. The field artillery was equipped with many old model M1877 field guns, though many batteries fielded the excellent and modern 76.2mm M1900

---

11 The 'bayonet' strength of a corps, however, was significantly fewer; around 28,000.
12 Menning, *Bayonets Before Bullets*, 110.

and M1902 Putilov guns. The Putilov guns had a longer range and fired at five times the rate of the older pieces. The Russians organized their field artillery into batteries of eight guns. Each army also had an assortment of heavy guns. The 2nd Manchurian Army had 100 such pieces, the 3rd Army in the centre had 140, while Linevich's 1st Manchurian Army possessed only 16 heavy pieces.

The Russians also had a clear advantage in cavalry at the battle of Mukden – 16,000 in total, more than twice as many 'sabres' as the Japanese. However, out of these, only three regiments were regular cavalry – dragoons. This comprised 18 *sotnias* (squadrons) out of the total of 114. The remaining 96 *sotnias*, or approximately 85 per cent of the cavalry force, were Cossack regiments, which were pulled from across the empire. These were of variable quality, but did not perform well during the Mukden campaign. They proved extremely casualty averse, and did not efficiently conduct reconnaissance or prove capable of delaying or disrupting Japanese manoeuvre. American observers noted that during the war, Japanese cavalry proved adept at dismounting behind one of the myriad walled villages that dotted Manchuria, and from these positions they were often effective at disrupting Russian advances. The Russian cavalry, especially on the right flank at Mukden, would prove incapable or unwilling to replicate this tactic. It should be noted, however, that Rennenkampf and Baumgarten effectively employed mixed infantry–cavalry forces on the eastern flank throughout the battle, implying that leadership at the brigade and division echelons was the decisive factor.

Russian 9in siege mortar in a fortified position north of San-de-pu. (Photo12/Ann Ronan Picture Library/Alamy Stock Photo)

JAPANESE

One of the more serious Russian miscalculations leading up to the war was the Russian War Ministry's underestimation of the scale of Japanese military potential. Prior to the conflict, the Russians estimated the total number of troops that Japan could mobilize for war at approximately 400,000, including reservists and territorial troops. This was not an altogether unreasonable estimate, considering that the strength of Japanese forces only nine years earlier in the 1894–95 Sino-Japanese War was no more than 60,000. However, in the intervening decade, the Japanese military and associated spending had rapidly expanded, and the organizational ability of the Japanese General Staff to raise and transport regiments to Asia would soon prove exceptional. These factors resulted in a total mobilization of nearly a million soldiers during the war, and the deployment of at least 670,000 of these to Manchuria. This was an astounding feat in a war that lasted only 18 months.

This scene doubtlessly played out hundreds of times at Mukden, as attacking infantry used inter-visibility lines (essentially, interim horizons) for cover. (Photo by Photo12/UIG/Getty Images)

Japanese Hotchkiss 6.5mm machine gun. At Mukden, batteries of six machine guns were distributed to support the regular infantry brigades. (Photo by George Rinhart/Corbis via Getty Images)

The Japanese did not employ the corps system perse, but instead deployed their forces to Asia in field armies, which in practice were only moderately larger than Russian corps. At Mukden, Oyama commanded five such armies, each generally consisting of three regular divisions, a cavalry brigade and one or more Kobi brigades (second-echelon reservists). Oyama also kept a 'general reserve' under his personal direction. At Mukden, it consisted of an infantry division and several Kobi brigades. There were only 13 regular army divisions at the time of Mukden, and all would serve with Oyama during the battle. Regular Japanese divisions consisted of two brigades made up of two regiments; regiments comprised three battalions, with each battalion made up of four 250-man companies.

By February 1905, nearly every Japanese regular division contained Kobi units. As noted by an American observer at the time, Kobi troops were the 'equivalent of *landwehr* in Europe'. They consisted of men who had served previously for seven-and-a-half years in the regular army, who were liable to be reactivated within ten years of discharge. The attrition of regulars and the first-echelon reservists in the battles of 1904 resulted in new regulars and reservists serving as replacements in the existing 12 Japanese divisions. The Kobi units therefore added much-needed mass to the Japanese field armies in 1905. While they were expected to be somewhat lesser-performing troops, neither Kuropatkin's nor other witnesses' accounts support this. One of the Kobi brigades in Kawamura's Yalu Army consisted of veterans of the war with China in 1894–95, and fought ferociously, as it was expected to. Kobi brigades sometimes included Kobi artillery and Kobi pioneers, while the Kobi Division in the Yalu Army even included a Kobi cavalry regiment. Kobi regiments consisted of only two battalions instead of the normal three.

The Japanese infantryman was armed with the Arisaka Type 30 1897 rifle, which fired a 6.5mm bullet. This factor informed the later Japanese decision to purchase Hotchkiss 6.5mm machine guns, thereby standardizing their ammunition type. The Arisaka had a five-round magazine, and the Japanese infantry were known for quickly expending large quantities of rifle ammunition, not always with a high level of accuracy. The Japanese brigades manned their machine guns with infantrymen from within the brigade. The Hotchkiss was fed by 50-round metal strips, rather than a 'belt' like the Russian Maxim. Some accounts praise the Hotchkiss' lighter weight and its reliability, while others reported that it frequently jammed. While the Maxim was much heavier, it had a superior rate of fire, which was also noted at the time. Japanese troops did employ some captured Maxims after the battle of the Yalu at the opening of the war. While the Japanese were inferior in total numbers of infantry, artillery and cavalry at Mukden, they did possess an advantage in total number of machine guns – over 254 compared to the Russians' 56. Like the Russians, the Japanese employed these exceptionally in defence, and were making progress towards effectively incorporating them to support infantry attacks.

Though few in number, the Japanese cavalry would fulfil its role at Mukden and prevent the Russian cavalry from interfering with the manoeuvre of the Japanese armies. (Author's collection)

Where the Japanese were known for their accuracy was in the employment of field artillery. The Type 31 (M1898) 75mm field gun was inferior to the Russian field piece, but the Japanese soldiers nonetheless put it to good effect. Russian officers commented with amazement on the speed at which Japanese artillery could rapidly 'walk' itself onto its targets. Captain Soloviev even noted incidences where a Japanese second or even first shell would land directly above a Russian formation, causing casualties before the soldiers even had a chance to go to ground or take cover. One-third of the Japanese artillery park consisted of mountain guns, which were lighter, shorter-range pieces that could be moved by a team of five pack ponies. These would prove effective in the fighting on the eastern flank at Mukden. Lastly, the Japanese possessed a substantial number of heavy howitzers, mortars and siege howitzers, of which the 28cm (11in) howitzers had just arrived in the Mukden lines, fresh from Port Arthur. Heavy mortars were organized into batteries of six guns like the field artillery, while the heavy howitzers were grouped in batteries of four and the 28cm howitzers in batteries of two guns.

The Japanese cavalry was a small force, but aggressive and effective at San-de-pu and Mukden. Organizationally, every division had one regiment (numbered in accordance with its division) of three squadrons assigned to it, with a squadron generally consisting of 100–150 troopers. The army also possessed two independent cavalry brigades, the 1st and 2nd, each consisting of two regiments of four squadrons. At Mukden, the Japanese had around 7,300 cavalry in total, which was barely enough to perform the necessary screening and reconnaissance roles, and not enough to be used in an exploitive role at the end of the battle.

Despite the heavy, even excessive, attrition of most Japanese units over the past nine months of fighting, they continued to display exceptional resilience and determination throughout the Mukden campaign. Oyama had ensured that replacements were fed into the front-line divisions to as great an extent as possible, bringing these armies up to regulation strength, or in the case of some companies up to as many as 300 men, greater than the 250 authorized.

ORDERS OF BATTLE, BATTLE OF MUKDEN (20 FEBRUARY 1905)

Numbers in parenthesis denote either battalions, squadrons or number of guns.
ESRR – East Siberian Rifle Regiment; Bn – battalion; Batt – Battery

Russian Manchurian Armies

Commander-in-chief: Gen Nikolaevich Kuropatkin – Chief of Staff: Lt Gen Sakharov
Quartermaster General: Maj Gen Evert

General Reserve (forces to be committed at commander-in-chief's discretion)

72nd Infantry Division: Maj Gen Radkevich (146th Tsaritsin Regiment) (4)
    1st Brigade: Maj Gen Bolotov (285th Mtsensk and 286th Kirsanov Regiments) (8)
    2nd Brigade: Maj Gen Kusov (287th Taruss and 288th Kulikov Regiments) (8)
    10th Artillery Brigade: 6 batteries (48 guns)

XVI Corps: Lt Gen Topornin

25nd Infantry Division: Lt Gen Pnevski
    1st Brigade: Maj Gen Klei (97th Lithuanian and 98th Yuriev Regiments) (8)
    2nd Brigade: (temporary) Col Prince Gedroits (99th Ivangorod Regiment) (4)
    25th Artillery Brigade: Maj Gen Pototski, 6 batteries (48 guns)
41st Infantry Division: Lt Gen Birger
    1st Brigade: Maj Gen Elliot (161st Alexandropol and 162nd Akhaltsikh Regiments) (8)
    45th Artillery Brigade: Maj Gen Bandrovski, 6 batteries (48 guns)
    10th Orenburg Cossacks (3 squadrons)
    16th Sapper Battalion (1 battalion)

General Reserve total: 40 infantry battalions, 3 squadrons, 1 sapper battalion, 144 guns; ~32,000 infantry, 360 sabres

1st Manchurian Army

Commander: Gen Linevich – Chief of Staff: Lt Gen Kharkevich

1st Manchurian Army Reserve
6th East Siberian Rifle Division: Maj Gen Danilov
    1st Brigade: Col Nekrasov (temporary) (21st ESRR and 22nd ESRR) (5)
    2nd Brigade: Col Kukuran (temporary) (23rd ESRR and 24th ESRR) (6)
7th and 8th Batteries, 26th Artillery Brigade (16 guns)
Machine Gun Company, 6th East Siberian Rifle Division (8 machine guns)

I Corps: Gen Baron Meiendorf, ADC

22nd Infantry Division: Lt Gen Fleisher
    1st Brigade: Maj Gen Novikov (85th Viborg and 86th Wilmandstrand Regiments) (8)
    2nd Brigade: Maj Gen Frish (87th Neishlot and 88th Petrov Regiments) (8)
    7th Artillery Brigade: Maj Gen Volkovitski, 5 Batteries (32 guns)
37th Infantry Division: Maj Gen Polzikov
    1st Brigade: Maj Gen Mandruika (145th Novocherkask Regiment Regiment) (4)
    2nd Brigade: Maj Gen Polzikov (147th Samara and 148th Caspian Regiments) (8)
    43rd Artillery Brigade: Maj Gen Kokhanov, 6 batteries (48 guns)
    2nd Brigade – 5th East Siberian Rifle Division: Maj Gen Putilov (19th ESRR and 20th ESRR) (6)
Corps assets:
Ussuri Cossack Regiment (2 squadrons), 1st Battery 2nd Siberian Artillery Division (8 old pattern guns)
3rd Trans-Baikal Cossack Battery (6 guns), 1st Sapper Battalion

4th Siberian Corps: Lt Gen Zarubaiev

2nd Siberian Infantry Division: Maj Gen Levestam
    1st Brigade: Col Danilchuk (5th Irkutsk and 6th Yeniseisk Regiments) (8)
    2nd Brigade: Maj Gen Oganovski (7th Krasnokarsk and 8th Tomsk Regiments) (8)
    1st Siberian Artillery Brigade: Col Vevern, 4 batteries (32 guns)
3rd Siberian Infantry Division: Maj Gen Shileiko
    1st Brigade: Col Dushkevich (temp) (9th Tobolsk and 10th Omsk Regiments) (8)
    2nd Brigade: Maj Gen Baron Rebinder (11th Semipalatinsk and 12th Barnaul Regiments) (8)
    26th Artillery Brigade: Maj Gen Aliev, 3 batteries (12 guns)
Corps assets:
2nd Verkhne-Udinsk Cossack Regiment, 7th Siberian Cossack Regiment (10 squadrons)
2nd Trans-Baikal Cossack Battery (6 guns)
1st Siberian Artillery Division: Col Kardinalovski (16 old pattern guns)
4th Battery, 5th East Siberian Artillery Bde (8 guns), 2nd Battery, 7th Artillery Bde (8 guns)
4th East Siberian Sapper Battalion

2nd Siberian Corps: Lt Gen Zasulich

5th East Siberian Rifle Division: Maj Gen Okulich (temporary)
    1st Brigade: Maj Gen Okulich (17th ESRR and 18th ESRR) (6)
    5th East Siberian Artillery Brigade: Maj Gen De Bruxes (18 guns)
1st Siberian Infantry Division: Maj Gen Morozov
    1st Brigade: Col Lobasov (temp) (1st Strietensk and 2nd Chita Regiments) (8)
    2nd Brigade: Maj Gen Istomin (3rd Nerchinsk and 4th Verkhne-Udinsk Regiments) (8)
    6th East Siberian Artillery Brigade: Col Meister, 3 batteries (24 guns)
Corps assets:
7th Siberian Cossack Regiment (2 squadrons), 4th Siberian Cossack Regiment (1)
5th East Siberian Mountain Battery (8 guns), half of 7th East Siberian Mount Batt (4)
2nd East Siberian Howitzer Battery (6), Machine Gun Co, 5th East Siberian Rifle Division (6)
3rd East Siberian Sapper Battalion

3rd Siberian Corps: Lt Gen Ivanov

3rd East Siberian Rifle Division: Maj Gen Kashtalinski
    1st Brigade: Maj Gen Mardanov (9th ESRR and 10th ESRR) (6)
    2nd Brigade: Col Tsuibulski (temp) (11th ESRR and 12th ESRR) (6)
    3rd East Siberian Artillery Brigade: Col Kalin (temporary), 4 batteries (32 guns)
    6th East Siberian Artillery Brigade, 1 battery (8 guns)
284th (Chembar) Regiment (4 battalions)
Siberian Cossack Cavalry Division: Maj Gen von Baumgarten (temporary)
    1st Brigade: (4th Siberian Cossack Regiment) (4 squadrons)
    2nd Brigade: (5th and 6th Siberian Cossack Regiments) (8)
Mounted Scout Detachment, 13th East Siberian Rifle Regiment (1 detachment)
4th and 6th East Siberian Mountain Batteries (16 guns)
3rd Horse Mountain Battery Frontier Guards (2 guns)
Machine Gun Co, 3rd East Siberian Rifle Division (6 x machine guns), 2nd East Siberian Sapper Bn (2 companies)

Chenghocheng Detachment: Lt Gen Pavel von Rennenkampf (originally Lt Gen Alexeiv)

71st Infantry Division: Lt Gen Ekk
    1st Brigade: Maj Gen Pogoretski (281st Drissa and 282nd Chernoyar Regiments) (7)
    2nd Brigade: Maj Gen Nudzhevski (283rd Bugulmin Regiment) (4)

6th Battery 26th Artillery Brigade, 1 battery (8 guns)
Composite Siberian Infantry Brigade: Maj Gen Maslov (6th Yeniseisk, 7th Krasnoyarsk, 9th Tobolsk and 10th Omsk Siberian Reserve Battalions) (4)
    2nd Battalion, 21st East Siberian Rifle Regiment (1 battalion)
    5th Trans-Baikal Cossack Infantry Battalion (1 battalion)
Trans-Baikal Cossack Cavalry Division
    1st Brigade: (2nd Chita Cossack Regiment) (5 squadrons)
    2nd Brigade: Maj Gen Liubavin (2nd Nerchinsk and 2nd Argun Cossack Regiments) (10)
3rd and 8th East Siberian Mountain Batteries (16 guns)
Horse Mountain Guns Frontier Guards (6 guns)
Part of 2nd and 3rd East Siberian Sapper Battalions (2½ companies)

1st Manchurian Army total: 133½ infantry battalions, 49 squadrons, 3 sapper battalions, 370 guns, 22 machine guns; ~98,946 infantry, 5,364 sabres

2nd Manchurian Army

Commander: Gen Baron Kaulbars – Chief of Staff: Lt Gen Ruzski
Cavalry Detachment: Maj Gen Grekov (originally Lt Gen Rennenkampf)
Ural Trans-Baikal Cossack Division: Maj Gen Pavlov (temporary)
    1st Brigade: (4th and 5th Ural Cossack Regiments) (9 squadrons)
    2nd Brigade: (1st Verkhne-Udinsk and 1st Chita Cossack Regiments) (11)
Caucasian Cavalry Brigade: Maj Gen Prince Orbeliani (Terek-Kuban and 2nd Dagestan Cavalry Regiments) (12 squadrons)
Orenburg Cossack Division (only 2½ squadrons located with Maj Gen Grekov's Detachment)
1st Trans-Baikal Cossack Battery (6 guns), 4th Trans-Baikal Artillery Battery (6)
10th Horse Artillery Div: Col Zhabuiko (20th and 11th Horse Art Battery) (12 guns)
3rd Don Cossack Artillery Division (2nd and 3rd Don Cossack Battery) (12 guns)

Provisional Rifle Corps: Lt Gen Kutnevich
1st Rifle Brigade: Maj Gen Dombrovski (1st, 2nd, 3rd and 4th Rifle Regiments) (8)
1st Rifle Artillery Division: Col Savalov, 3 batteries (24 guns)
2nd Rifle Brigade: Maj Gen Petrov (5th, 6th, 7th and 8th Rifle Regiments) (8)
2nd Rifle Artillery Division: Col Kotsarevski, 3 batteries (24 guns)
5th Rifle Brigade: Maj Gen Churin (17th, 18th, 19th and 20th Rifle Regiments) (8)
5th Rifle Artillery Division: Col Pryaslov, 3 batteries (24 guns)
1st Orenburg Cossack Regiment (3 squadrons)
1st Battery of the 3rd and 1st of the 4th Siberian Artillery Div (16 old pattern guns)
1st Battery, 5th Howitzer Regiment (6 guns), 3rd Battery, 5th Howitzer Regiment (6)
Machine Gun Co, 1st East Siberian Rifle Div (8 machine guns) and Co of 2nd East Siberian Rifle Division (8 machine guns)
Half Machine Gun Company, 9th East Siberian Rifle Division (4 machine guns)
1st East Siberian Sapper Battalion (1½ companies)

VIII Corps: Lt Gen Muilov
14th Infantry Division: Lt Gen Rusanov
    1st Brigade: Maj Gen Glyebov (53rd Volhynia and 54th Misk Regiments) (7)
    2nd Brigade: Maj Gen Ganenfeldt (55th Podolia and 56th Jitomir Regiments) (8)
    41st Artillery Brigade: Maj Gen Mingin, 6 batteries (48 guns)
15th Infantry Division: Lt Gen Ivanov
    1st Brigade: Maj Gen Nekrasov (57th Modlin and 58th Praga Regiments) (8)
    2nd Brigade: Maj Gen Golembatovski (59th Liublin and 60th Zamostye Regiments) (8)
29th Artillery Brigade: Col Bazarevski, 6 batteries (48 guns)

1st and 11th Orenburg Cossack Regiments (3 squadrons)
2nd Batt, 3rd Siberian Artillery Division (8 old pattern guns), 2nd Batt, 4th Sib Art Div (8)
9th East Siberian Mountain Battery, 1 battery (8 guns)
1st East Siberian Howitzer Battery (6 guns), 2nd Battery, 5th Howitzer Regiment (6)
12th Sapper Battalion (1 company)

X Corps: Lt Gen Tserpitski
9th Infantry Division: Lt Gen Gershelmann
    1st Brigade: Maj Gen Zhdanovski (33rd Elets and 34th Syev Regiments) (8)
    2nd Brigade: Maj Gen Shatilov (35th Bryansk and 36th Orel Regiments) (8)
    9th Artillery Brigade: Col Sukhinski, 3 batteries (24 guns)
31st Infantry Division: Maj Gen Vasilev
    1st Brigade: Maj Gen Chizhevich (121st Penza and 122 Tambov Regiments) (8)
    2nd Brigade: Maj Gen Vasilev (123rd Koslov and 124th Voronej Regiments) (8)
31st Artillery Brigade: Maj Gen Kosinski, 6 batteries (48 guns)
Corps assets:
1st Orenburg Cossack Regiment (1 squadron)
2nd Battery, 2nd Siberian Artillery Division, 1 battery (8 old pattern guns)
10th East Siberian Mountain Battery, 1 battery (8 guns)
3rd Battery, 4th Howitzer Regiment (6 guns), 4th Battery, 5th Howitzer Regiment (6)
6th Sapper Battalion (1 company)

1st Siberian Corps: Lt Gen Gerngross
1st East Siberian Rifle Division: Maj Gen Dovbor-Musnitski (temp)
    1st Brigade: Col Lesh (temp) (1st ESSR, 2nd ESRR) (6)
    2nd Brigade: Maj Gen Suichevski (3rd ESRR and 4th ESRR) (6)
    1st East Siberian Artillery Brigade: Maj Gen Luchkovski, 4 batteries (32 guns)
9th East Siberian Rifle Division: Maj Gen Krause (temp)
    1st Brigade: Maj Gen Krause (33rd ESRR and 34th ESRR) (6)
    2nd Brigade: Maj Gen Bachinski (temp) (35th ESRR and 36th ESRR) (6)
    9th East Siberian Artillery Brigade: Maj Gen Mrozovski, 4 batteries (31 guns)
Corps assets:
Primorsk Dragoon Regiment (6 squadrons)
Half Machine Gun Company, 9th East Siberian Rifle Division (4 machine guns)
1st East Siberian Sapper Battalion (2½ companies)

2nd Manchurian Army total: 120 infantry battalions, 79 squadrons, 3 sapper battalions, 439 guns, 24 machine guns; ~80,799 infantry, 7,990 sabres

3rd Manchurian Army

Commander: Gen Baron Bilderling (temp) – Chief of Staff: Lt Gen Martsen
5th Siberian Corps: Lt Gen Dembovski
54th Infantry Division: Artamonov
    1st Brigade: Maj Gen Peterov (213th Orovai and 214th Mokshan Regiments) (8)
    2nd Brigade: Maj Gen Lisovski (216th Insar Regiment) (4)
    28th Artillery Brigade: Maj Gen Putintsev, 5 batteries (40 guns)
61st Infantry Division: Maj Gen Podvalnyuk
    1st Brigade: Maj Gen Pryaslov (242nd Belebeev Regiment) (4)
    2nd Brigade: Col Apukhtin (temp) (243rd Zlatoust and 244th Borisov Regiments) (8)
    40th Artillery Brigade: Maj Gen Slezkin, 6 batteries (48 guns)
Corps assets:
1st Argun Cossack Regiment (4 squadrons)
4th Battery, 4th Howitzer Regiment, 1 battery (6 guns)
Unattached Machine Gun Companies (10 machine guns)
5th East Siberian Sapper Battalion (1 company)

XVI Corps: Lt Gen Selivanov
3rd Infantry Division: Maj Gen Orlov
    1st Brigade: Maj Gen Zashchuk (9th Ingermanland and 10th Novoingermanland Regiments) (8)
    2nd Brigade: Maj Gen De Vitt (11th Pskov and 12th Velikolutsk Regiments) (8)
    3rd Artillery Brigade: Maj Gen Gribunin, 6 batteries (48 guns)
35th Infantry Division: Maj Gen Dobrzhinski
    1st Brigade: Maj Gen Glinski (137th Nyejin and 138th Bokhov Regiments) (8)
    2nd Brigade: Maj Gen Glasko (139th Morshansk and 140th Zaraisk Regiments) (8)
    35th Artillery Brigade: Maj Gen Terpilovski, 6 batteries (48 guns)
Corps assets:
1st Battery, 4th Howitzer Regiment (6 guns)
17th Sapper Battalion (1 company)

6th Siberian Corps: Lt Gen Sobolev
55th Infantry Division: Maj Gen Laiming
    1st Brigade: Maj Gen Frankovski (217th Krom and 218th Korisoglyebsk Regiments) (8)
    2nd Brigade: Col Ponomarev (219th Yukhnov and 220th Yepifan Regiments) (8)
    6th Artillery Brigade: Maj Gen Kraevski, 6 batteries (48 guns)
Corps assets:
10th Orenburg Cossack Regiment (3 squadrons)
4th and 5th Old Pattern Field Artillery Batteries, 2 batteries (16 guns)
2nd Battery, 4th Howitzer Regiment, 1 battery (6 guns)
6th East Siberian Sapper Battalion (1 company)

3rd Manchurian Army total: 72 infantry battalions, 19 squadrons, 3 sapper battalions, 266 guns, 10 machine guns; ~56,773 infantry, 2,688 sabres

Total Russian Forces Available to Kuropatkin at Mukden: 275,666 bayonets (infantrymen), 16,382 sabres (cavalrymen), 1,219 guns (1,087 field, 72 mountain, 60 howitzer), 56 machine guns, 10 7/8 sapper battalions

JAPANESE

1st Army

Commander: Gen Baron Kuroki – Chief of Staff: Maj Gen Fuji
Guards Division: Lt Gen Asada
    1st Guard Brigade: Maj Gen Kimoura (1st and 2nd Guard Regiments) (6)
    2nd Guard Brigade: Maj Gen Watanabe (3rd and 4th Guard Regiments) (6)
    Guard Field Artillery Regiment, 6 batteries (36 guns)
    Captured Gun Detachment, 3 batteries (12 guns)
    18 x machine guns
    Guard Cavalry Regiment (2 squadrons)
    Guard Pioneer Battalion
    Guard Kobi Brigade (Maj Gen Umezawa) (1st, 2nd and 4th Guard Kobi Regiments) (6)
    Guard Kobi Cavalry (1 squadron)
    Guard Kobi Battery (6 guns)
    Kobi Pioneers (1 company)
    6 machine guns

12th Infantry Division: Lt Gen Inouye
    23rd Infantry Brigade: Maj Gen Shimamura (14th and 47th Infantry Regiments) (6)
    12th Infantry Brigade: Maj Gen Imamura (21st and 46th Infantry Regiments) (6)
    12th Cavalry Regiment (3 squadrons)
    12th Field Artillery Regiment, 6 batteries (36 guns)
    12th Engineer Battalion (1)
    12 x machine guns
    5th Kobi Brigade: Maj Gen Awaibara (21st, 11th and 42nd Kobi Regiments) (6)

2nd Infantry Division: Lt Gen Baron Nishijima
    3rd Infantry Brigade: Maj Gen Ishibashi (4th and 29th Infantry Regiments) (6)
    15th Infantry Brigade: Maj Gen Ohara (16th and 30th Infantry Regiments) (6)
    2nd Cavalry Regiment (3 squadrons)
    2nd Artillery Regiment, 6 batteries (36 guns)
    2nd Engineer Battalion (1)
    18 x machine guns
    29th Kobi Infantry Regiment (2), 39th Kobi Infantry Regiment (2)

12cm Artillery Battery (4 guns), 15cm Artillery Battery (4 guns)
9cm Mortar Battery (18 guns)
12th Pioneer Battalion

1st Army assets:
1st Battalion (3rd and 5th Batteries), 1st Heavy Artillery Regiment
    (1 battery, 4 x 4.7in guns; 1 battery, 4 x 5.9in guns)
2nd Independent Heavy Artillery Battalion (less 2nd Battery) (3 batteries, 18 x 3.5in guns)
1st Independent Battalion Kobi Field Artillery (3 batteries, 18 guns).
2 field guns, 2 captured Russian guns

1st Army total: 52 battalions, 10 squadrons, 174 guns, 54 machine guns, 10 engineer companies; ~55,858 men

2nd Army

Commander: Gen Baron Oku – Chief of Staff: Col Nitahara
8th Infantry Division: Lt Gen Baron Tatsumi
    4th Infantry Brigade: Maj Gen Yoda (5th and 31st Infantry Regiments) (6)
    16th Infantry Brigade: Maj Gen Kamada (17th and 32nd Infantry Regiments) (6)
    8th Cavalry Regiment (3 squadrons)
    8th Artillery Regiment, 6 batteries (36 mountain guns)
    8th Engineer Battalion

5th Infantry Division: Lt Gen Kigoshi
    9th Infantry Brigade: Maj Gen Suizama (11th and 41st Infantry Regiments) (6)
    21st Infantry Brigade: Maj Gen Murayama (21st and 42nd Infantry Regiments) (6)
    5th Cavalry Regiment (3 squadrons)
    5th Artillery Regiment, 6 batteries (36 guns)
    5th Engineer Battalion (1 battalion)
    5 x machine guns

4th Infantry Division: Lt Gen Baron Tsukamoto
    7th Infantry Brigade: Maj Gen Sunaga (8th and 37th Infantry Regiments) (6)
    19th Infantry Brigade: Maj Gen Hayashi (9th and 38th Infantry Regiments) (6)
    4th Cavalry Regiment (3 squadrons)
    4th Artillery Regiment, 6 batteries (36 guns)
    3 Independent Field Artillery Batteries
    4th Engineer Battalion (1)
    4 x machine guns

Tomioka Detachment: Col Tomioka
    8th Kobi Brigade (5th, 17th and 31st Kobi Regiments)
    34th Regiment (3)
    1 x Section Cavalry
    1 Brigade Field Artillery, 3 batteries (18 guns)
    1 captured battery (6 guns)
    1 Battery 3.5in. Mortars (4 guns)
    1 Company of Engineers
    3 battalions of infantry

2nd Army assets:
2nd Kobi Regiment (2 battalions)

6th Cavalry Regiment (2 squadrons), 3rd Cavalry Regiment (2½ squadrons)
13th Field Artillery Regiment, 6 batteries (36 guns)
2nd, 3rd and 4th Indep Battalion Kobi Field Artillery, 9 batteries (54 guns)
Field Heavy Artillery Regiment (4.7in howitzers), 4 batteries (24 guns)
2nd Bn 1st Heavy Artillery, 2nd Bn 2nd Heavy Artillery (5.9in), 4 batteries (24 guns)
2nd Battery, 2nd Independent Heavy Artillery Bn (3.5in mortars) (2 guns)
Captured Russian guns (10), Captured Russian 5.9in mortars (4)
Machine guns (27)

2nd Army total: 45 battalions, 21 squadrons, 278 guns, 47 machine guns, 9 engineer companies; ~53,809 men

3rd Army

Commander: Gen Baron Nogi – Chief of Staff: Maj Gen Matsunaga
  1st Infantry Division: Lt Gen Iida
    1st Infantry Brigade: Maj Gen Baba (1st and 15th Infantry Regiments) (6)
    2nd Infantry Brigade: Maj Gen Nakamura (2nd and 3rd Infantry Regiments) (6)
    1st Field Artillery Regiment, 6 batteries (36 guns)
    1st Cavalry Regiment (3 squadrons)
    1st Engineer Battalion (1)
    24 x machine guns

  7th Infantry Division: Lt Gen Baron Oseko
    13th Infantry Brigade: Maj Gen Yoshida (25th and 26th Infantry Regiments) (6)
    14th Infantry Brigade: Maj Gen Saite (27th and 28th Infantry Regiments) (6)
    7th Field Artillery Regiment, 4 batteries (12 field and 12 mountain guns)
    7th Cavalry Regiment (1¾ squadrons)
    7th Engineer Battalion (2 companies)
    15 x machine guns

  9th Infantry Division: Lt Gen Oshima
    6th Infantry Brigade: Maj Gen Ichinohe (7th and 35th Infantry Regiments) (6)
    18th Infantry Brigade: Maj Gen Hirasa (19th and 36th Infantry Regiments) (6)
    9th Field Artillery Regiment, 6 batteries (36 mountain guns)
    9th Cavalry Regiment (3 squadrons)
    9th Engineer Battalion (1)
    18 x machine guns
    2nd Cavalry Brigade (15th and 16th Cavalry Regiments) (8 squadrons; 6 x machine guns)

3rd Army assets:
2nd Field Artillery Brigade (16th, 17th and 18th Field Artillery Batteries) (72 guns)
15th Kobi Brigade (57th and 54th Kobi Regiments) (5)
6 captured Russian guns

3rd Army total: 41 battalions, 15¾ squadrons, 174 guns, 63 machine guns, 8 engineer companies; ~40,522 men

4th Army

Commander: Gen Count Nodzu – Chief of Staff: Maj Gen Uehara
  6th Division: Lt Gen Baron Okubo
    11th Brigade: Maj Gen Ishiwara (13th and 45th Infantry Regiments) (6)
    24th Brigade: Maj Gen Kagawa (23rd and 48th Infantry Regiments) (6)
    6th Cavalry Regiment (1 cavalron)
    6th Field Artillery, 6 batteries (36 guns)
    6th Engineer Battalion (1)
    18 x machine guns

  The Okubo Kobi Division: Maj Gen Okubo
    3rd Kobi Brigade (6th, 18th and 34th Kobi Regiments) (6)
    10th Kobi Brigade: Col Moji (10th, 20th and 40th Kobi Regiments) (6)
    11th Kobi Brigade: Maj Gen Oki (12th, 22nd and 43rd Kobi Regiments) (6)

  10th Division: Lt Gen Ando
    8th Brigade: Maj Gen Otami (10th and 40th Infantry Regiments) (6)
    20th Brigade: Maj Gen Okasaki (20th and 39th Infantry Regiments) (6)
    10th Cavalry Regiment (3 squadrons)
    10th Artillery Regiment, 6 batteries (36 mountain guns)
    10th Engineer Battalion (1)
    20 x machine guns

4th Army assets:
2nd BN, 46th Kobi Regiment (1)
1st Battalion 1st Heavy Artillery Regiment, 3 batteries (12 guns)
2nd Heavy Artillery Regiment, 6 batteries 5.9in (36 guns)
4th Heavy Artillery Regiment, 6 batteries 3.5in (36 guns)
14 captured Russian guns, 4 captured Russian 3.9in guns, 6 x 11in howitzers
Kobi Engineers (1 company), 1st Field Artillery Brigade (14th and 15th Regiments), 6 batteries (72 guns)
16 x machine guns

4th Army total: 43 battalions, 4 squadrons, 252 guns, 54 machine guns, 7 engineer companies; ~49,575 men

5th (Yalu) Army

Commander: Lt Gen Kawamura – Chief of Staff: Maj Gen Uchiyama
  1st Kobi Division: Lt Gen Sasaki
    6th Kobi Brigade (13th, 23rd and 48th Kobi Regiments) (6)
    9th Kobi Brigade (7th, 19th and 36th Kobi Regiments) (6)
    Kobi Cavalry Regiment (2¾ squadrons)
    Kobi Artillery Regiment, 6 batteries (30 mountain guns)
    Kobi Engineer Battalion (1)
    12 x machine guns

  11th Division: Lt Gen Samejima
    10th Brigade: Maj Gen Yamanaka (22nd and 44th Infantry Regiments) (6)
    22nd Brigade: Maj Gen Mayeda (12th and 43rd Infantry Regiments) (6)
    11th Cavalry Regiment (3 squadrons)
    11th Artillery Regiment, 6 batteries (36 mountain guns)
    11th Engineer Battalion (1)
    24 x machine guns

5th Army assets:
16th Kobi Brigade, 2 Regiments (4¾)
59th Kobi Regiment (3)
1st Independent Battalion Heavy Artillery (3.5in mortars), 2 batteries (12 guns)

5th Army total: 31¾ battalions, 5¾ squadrons, 78 guns, 36 machine guns, 6 engineer companies; ~27,502 men

General Reserve

3rd Division: Lt Gen Baron Oshima
  5th Brigade: Maj Gen Nambo (6th and 33rd Infantry Regiments) (6)
  17th Brigade: Maj Gen Kodama (18th Infantry Regiment) (3)
  3rd Cavalry Regiment (half squadron), 3rd Artillery, 6 batteries (36 guns)
  3rd Engineer Battalion (1)
  1st Kobi Brigade (1st, 15th and 16th Kobi Regiments) (6)
  13th Kobi Brigade (51st and 52nd Kobi Regiments) (4)
  14th Kobi Brigade (35th and 40th Kobi Regiments) (6)

General Reserve total: 27 battalions, ¾ squadrons, 36 guns, 3 engineer companies; ~22,543 men

Total Japanese Forces Available to Oyama at Mukden: 199,254 infantry, 7,353 cavalry, 32,877 artillerymen, 1,614 machine gunners, 8,717 engineers. Total – 249,815 men, 992 guns, 254 machine guns

OPPOSING PLANS

RUSSIAN

In the days following San-de-pu, Kuropatkin, becoming concerned about threats to the strategic rail line deep in the Russian rear, began tasking units from his field armies to deal with these concerns. In all, these units amounted to a significant force, with eight battalions of infantry and 36 squadrons of cavalry, as well as 10,000 'draftees' who would have been replacements for casualties in the field armies. These troops were supplementing many tens of thousands of Russians who were already guarding the Trans-Siberian Railway – over 50,000 men in total. In addition to highlighting the practical problems arising from fighting a war at the end of the longest ground line of supply in history, this drain on manpower lowered the strength of the Russian forces at the looming battle for Mukden. While the threats to Kuropatkin's lines of supply, communication and strategic rear were not inconsequential, the magnitude of his response to these dangers prioritized rear security.

Kuropatkin may have committed too many troops to guarding the railroad – up to 50,000. However, incidents of attempted sabotage were widely reported. (Author's collection)

In prioritizing and mitigating risk to his rear echelons and lines of supply, he likewise increased the risk to his field armies. Despite receiving some 70,000 additional Russian troops in the theatre of operations between the battles of San-de-pu and Mukden, only a minority of these would make their way to the armies at Mukden.

After the battle of San-de-pu, Kuropatkin feared an imminent Japanese attack, possibly one that incorporated Nogi's 3rd Army. Kuropatkin therefore prepared his armies for defensive operations for three days, from 29–31 January. When no attack took place, Kuropatkin decided on 1 February to begin once again to prepare for his own offensive. None of Nogi's units had so far been detected anywhere along the front, and while the Russians suspected that perhaps some had arrived, the bulk of the Japanese 3rd Army were thought to still be in transit. Inexplicably, Kuropatkin did not solicit his subordinates for their opinions related to the coming offensive until 12 February, and then did not definitively decide on a course of action until he held a council of war on 19 February. All the Russian army commanders were in agreement that the offensive should recommence at once, and that its object should be the Japanese left flank – again in the vicinity of San-de-pu. Kaulbars for one hoped that this time, the 1st and 3rd Manchurian Armies would actively support the 2nd (which he now commanded) and this would allow for the pressure and dilemmas that Kuropatkin had failed to force on Oyama in the last battle. Additionally, Kuropatkin seemed predisposed to better support the next battle for San-de-pu with additional divisions or even corps from the sizeable General Reserve that he had assembled. Prior to the battle of Mukden, Kuropatkin held under his personal command the XVI Corps under Gen Topornin, the 72nd Division of the 6th Siberian Corps and the 146th 'Tsaritsin' Regiment of I Corps. Unfortunately, the nearly unanimous decision of the generals for a renewed offensive did not result in orders being issued until 21 February, a further delay of two days. On the next day, Kaulbars issued orders to 2nd Manchurian Army, ordering a complete day of rest on the 23rd, preparations for attack on the 24th and the actual attack to commence on 25 February. It took Kuropatkin and the Russian staff system three-and-a-half weeks to pull itself out of its post-San-de-pu stupor and into action – at which point, events had overtaken them.

Contemporary illustration of Russian infantry in combat at Mukden. (Author's collection)

Kuropatkin is thought to be the first commander of an army in combat to use an automobile when inspecting positions. (Album/Alamy Stock Photo)

JAPANESE

After the battle of the Sha-Ho in October 1904, the Japanese armies deliberately minimized the construction of complex obstacles to their front. Oyama instructed his generals to ensure that their defensive preparations did not impede their future offensive operations. For this reason, Japanese entrenchments were relatively simple, often consisting of a simple forward trench line, with only redoubts and fortified villages adding depth. The Japanese left large areas to the front of their battle positions bereft of wire obstacles and other barriers, ensuring that they would have clear lanes through which to attack when the time came.

In the centre of the Japanese lines, this minimal approach was not altogether possible. Here, south of Mukden where the Russian 3rd Manchurian Army faced most of Nodzu's 4th and Kuroki's 1st Armies, the density of forces on each side was higher, and the distance between the opposing armies was narrower; in many places as few as 300m, and at the widest only about 1km. Opposite the Japanese centre, the Russians were concentrated at a density of a corps for every 6km, while on the flanks, the Russians were twice or even three times as dispersed. Consequently, a breakthrough in the centre of the battlefield would likely require a brutal frontal attack through masses of obstacles and fortifications. The Russians had in fact suffered some disruption in the battle of San-de-pu in 'breaking out' of their own wire- and obstacle-laden positions. Determined to avoid this, Oyama's right and left flanks were less encumbered by heavy wire, mines and other obstacles.

This disposition fitted with the operational plans for the coming battle at Mukden. Essentially, Oyama's plan was to convince Kuropatkin that the Japanese were seeking to decisively envelop the Russian left (western) flank. Once Kuropatkin committed his reserves there, the Japanese main effort would envelop the Russian right flank instead. The length of the battlefield, 145km by 28 February, would preclude the Russians from easily transferring forces. In practice, this would be impossible anyway due to the intensity of attacks by all of the Japanese armies along the front.

In order to be successful, Oyama's plan needed to convince the Russian high command that the fighting that would soon break out in the east was truly the main effort. In other words, Kawamura's Yalu Army would have to 'sell' the attack on the Russian left. To successfully accomplish this required the attack to begin in advance of the main envelopment on the Russian right, and for the diversionary attack to be conducted with the utmost intensity and aggression, so that the Russians believed it to be the Japanese main attack. Lastly and most importantly, Kuropatkin needed to be convinced that the diversionary attack consisted of Nogi's long-awaited veterans, fresh from their victory at Port Arthur.

To this end, Oyama had a month earlier organized Kawamura's 5th Army around the Japanese 11th Division of Nogi's 3rd Army. In addition to the veteran regulars of the 11th Division, Kawamura had the 1st Kobi Division and an additional four Kobi regiments. In total, the new army consisted of 12 regular battalions, 20 Kobi battalions, 18 machine guns, six squadrons of cavalry and 60 cannons.

Once Kuropatkin detected the veterans of the Japanese 11th Division, formerly of Nogi's Army, but now with Kawamura, Oyama believed Kuropatkin could be tricked into committing his reserves to the eastern flank. Meanwhile, Nogi's actual 3rd Army would attack in the west, executing a deep envelopment. Even without the 11th Division, Nogi's 3rd Army was still equal in strength to the other armies. It now consisted of the 1st, 7th, and 9th Divisions, as well as four Kobi battalions, for a total of 40 battalions, 36 machine guns, nine squadrons of cavalry and 216 field guns.

Meanwhile, the centre armies, especially Nodzu's 4th Army, were expected to be less mobile. Oku's 2nd Army would protect Nogi's flank, assisting the 3rd Army as needed, while Kuroki would help Kawamura in a similar way in the east. Nodzu would merely defend, though keeping the Russians to his front alert by conducting the heaviest artillery bombardments of the war.

Executed perfectly, Kuropatkin would first be convinced that the Japanese were turning his eastern flank, where he would transfer the preponderance of his reserves, while the actual attack would envelop his right. Ideally, the Russian superiority of numbers would be negated by the frequent deployment and redeployment of troops, which would reduce the actual forces in contact with the Japanese to rough parity. This would be crucial, as Oyama was essentially attempting to replicate the 1870 Prussian victory of Sedan. Oyama's chief of staff, Gen Kodama, confirmed this point after the battle, stating that Oyama's objective at Mukden had been the destruction of the Russian field forces, not merely a battlefield victory that pushed the Russians further north.

The Japanese staff issued its official orders to the armies on 20 February. Kawamura would begin moving immediately from his position some 40km south-east of the Japanese 1st Army. They would need to be in position to attack the forward Russian position near Chenghocheng beginning on the 23rd. Meanwhile, Kuroki's 1st Army would begin attacking no later than 27 February, supporting Kawamura and further conveying the message to the Russians that the east was the decisive front. The 4th and 2nd Armies would remain in place for the time being, while on the far left of the Japanese lines, Nogi's 3rd Army would not begin its advance until 26 February, three days after the initiation on the opposite flank. It was likely that it would be a day or two before Nogi's 3rd Army would be positively identified by Russian cavalry, corresponding to approximately 28 February – at which point the Japanese plan would be revealed.

THE CAMPAIGN

THE BATTLEFIELD

The battlefield of Mukden was bisected by a north–south rail line running just west of the city of Mukden. To the west of the rail line, the country was exceptionally flat and barren. While dotted by myriad walled towns and villages, the landscape was otherwise nearly devoid of features, as the trees had been denuded long ago due to the needs of the densely populated local area.

East of the rail line, there was about 15km of gradually more complex terrain, generally consisting of a few prominent hills with accompanying spurs and gullies, while the majority of the landscape was still flat or rolling. Two of these hills, Putilov Hill and Novgorod Hill, located just south of the Sha-Ho River, had already been fought over in the October battle of the Sha-Ho. It was also here that both sides, but especially the Russians, had their most intricate fortifications and trench systems. Around 15km east of the city of Mukden, the country becomes exceptionally rough and steep, with fewer settlements, especially on heights, though the terrain is still mostly devoid of woods.

From north to south, the battlefield can be understood in relation to the major rivers. As previously stated, after the battle of the Sha-Ho, the armies remained essentially in place. These initial positions faced each other across the Sha-Ho River. In the west, however, around Hei-kou-tai and San-de-pu, a further, much larger river ran north-east–south-west. This river, the Hun-Ho, passes just south of the city of Mukden, about 10km north of the Sha-Ho defensive positions. Kuropatkin had ordered a second defensive line constructed here in the winter months. Therefore, the Russians had a subsequent defensive position to fall back to, in the event they were outfought along the Sha-Ho.

A victim of accurate Russian artillery. This photograph gives a good impression of the barren Manchurian landscape. (Author's collection)

PHASE I – DIVERSION, 19–26 FEBRUARY

The diversion – Kawamura attacks in the east

The Russians experienced one further shuffling of commanders during the weeks prior to the battle of Mukden, this time involving the cavalry. The commander of the cavalry corps on the right, Gen Mishchenko, had suffered a wounded foot during the battle of San-de-pu, so on 9 February, Gen von Rennenkampf, previously commanding the Chenghocheng Detachment on the left, took over from him on the western flank. The Chenghocheng Detachment was a mixed infantry, cavalry and artillery force, initially slightly larger than a division, whose mission was to screen dozens of kilometres of rough terrain to the east and south-east of the main Russian lines at Mukden.

Once in command of the cavalry corps on the Russian right, Rennenkampf was ordered to secure this flank by clearing the western side of the Hun-Ho River of any Japanese infantry and cavalry who had established themselves there after the battle of San-de-pu. With four cavalry brigades, Rennenkampf executed this task energetically and competently from 14–16 February, but was soon forced to give up two of his brigades to higher headquarters. These brigades would be dispatched north by Kuropatkin to secure the strategic rail line as described previously.

Rennenkampf was a capable commander who, perhaps more than any other Russian senior commander, would actively seek to locate, report on and neutralize enemy efforts in whichever sector of the battlefield where he was in command. Kuropatkin's original reason for replacing the wounded Mishchenko with the highly competent Rennenkampf was to prepare this flank for the planned Russian offensive. The fact that, from 17–23 February, he was in the right place to detect and delay Nogi's decisive assault would prove tragic for the Russians, as he would soon be transferred back to the Russian left, once Kuropatkin began to worry about Kawamura's developing offensive.

Meanwhile, on the eastern flank, the new commander of the Chenghocheng Detachment was Gen Alexeiv. The detachment's purpose was to extend the Russian lines far beyond the main positions of 1st Manchurian Army along the Sha-Ho, enabling coverage of some additional 30km to the south-east. This would provide early warning and reaction time should the Japanese attempt a deep envelopment. This part of the Russian line was not continuous, however. Rather, Alexeiv's force was established in one regimental-size position under Gen Liubavin in a blocking position complete with redoubts, some 15km out from the main Russian lines. The main force under Gen Ekk was a further 10km east and forward of Liubavin's position. Ekk arrayed his force on several hills near the village of Chenghocheng, covering the key passes through this part of the battlefield. The kilometres in between each element consisted of severely restrictive terrain.

Putilov Hill held against the Japanese counter-attack at the battle of the Sha-Ho, and would hold again at Mukden. (Sueddeutsche Zeitung Photo/Alamy Stock Photo)

Kawamura's 5th (Yalu) Army began its advance on the night of 18/19 February from the village of Piao-tsy-iuan, to reach the start point assigned to it prior to the actual date of attack on 23 February. The Yalu Army had 20km to advance to its start point, and it would be doing so through narrow passes in the rough terrain of this part of the battlefield, likely in the face of forward Russian cavalry detachments and isolated infantry outposts. The army began its march in two separate advancing columns, the 11th Division on the left and Kobi Division to the right. On the 19th, the Japanese columns made steady progress, encountering only small cavalry reconnaissance detachments along the way, reaching the village of Nan-dian-tsy, close to their start-point by 20 February. On the 20th, some eight battalions and 12 guns of Kawamura's force conducted a probing attack on the Russian Chenghocheng Detachment, pushing back some forward positions.

On the 20th, Alexeiv realized he was facing at least a locally important Japanese attack, and notified his immediate superior, 1st Manchurian Army's Gen Linevich. Linevich immediately dispatched a regiment of the 6th East Siberian Rifle Division and four machine guns from his reserve, and sent them to Alexeiv. On 21 February, the Japanese Yalu Army and Russian Chenghocheng Detachment confined themselves to firing artillery at each other's known and suspected positions, but did not make any concerted attacks. By 22 February, Alexeiv, having received his regiment of reinforcements and machine guns, attacked the Japanese Kobi Division and 11th Division column across his immediate front.

Alexeiv conducted his attack in four columns, each about two battalions strong. The ground was exceptionally icy and the day was bitterly cold, resulting in the columns making slow progress through the hills. By midmorning, they encountered several Kobi regiments with supporting artillery, which quickly opened fire. The Russian attack was not very spirited, and the Russian columns soon broke contact after suffering about 150 casualties. Alexeiv consolidated his detachment in its original defensive positions around Chenghocheng, where they prepared for a Japanese attack with entrenchments on high ground and obstacles to their front.

On 23 February, with a severe snowstorm beginning, the Japanese 11th Division and 1st Kobi Division attacked the Chenghocheng Detachment in strength. One position, located on Beresnev Hill, exemplified the day's fighting. The hill was defended by two companies of Russian infantry, a dismounted squadron and two machine guns. The Russians were entrenched on the summit of the hill, with sandbag parapets for their rifles and wire entanglements across their front. The eastern slope of the hill was a strongpoint, with a redoubt anchoring the position. Unlike the Russians on the previous day, the Japanese 9th Kobi Brigade attacked Beresnev Hill with notable fervour. Several Japanese batteries placed heavy fire on the summit of the hill, supporting the Japanese Kobi infantry who soon rushed up the slope. Each man carried a sandbag to establish a firing position once his unit began to take suppressive fire. Though the Japanese eventually made their way in and among the Russian wire obstacles, which they began to tear out of the ground, they were soon thrown back by defensive fire. At 2130hrs and again at around 2300hrs, the 9th Kobi Brigade attacked twice more, but was pushed back each time, establishing positions 200m from the obstacles for the rest of the night. The 6th Kobi Brigade had a similar experience at the nearby Deniken Hill.

Eastern flank of the battlefield, 19–28 February 1905

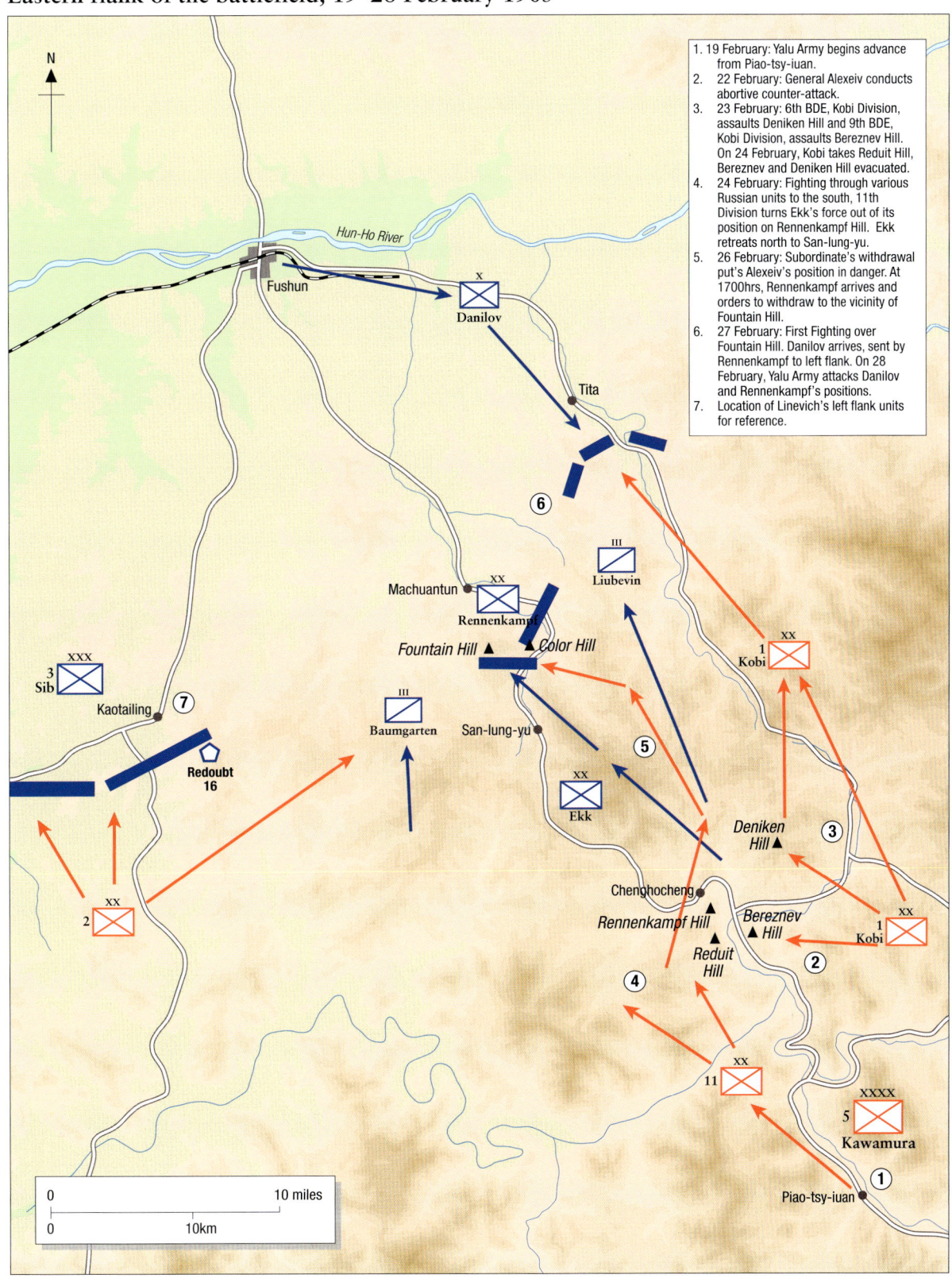

On 24 February, the Japanese renewed their attack with equal determination, bombarding the sector around Beresnev Hill with several batteries. Meanwhile, parts of the 9th Kobi Brigade, with help from infantry and sappers from the 11th Division, were able to storm Reduit Hill to the south-west of Beresnev, while attacks continued on Deniken Hill. In short order, the Japanese began firing from multiple hilltops on the Russian position at Beresnev Hill, causing the survivors of the detachment to retreat with their wounded commander, Lieutenant Colonel (Lt Col) Beresnev. The Russians all began to withdraw to the next line of heights, centred on Rennenkampf Hill, where the survivors of the day's fighting were supported and received by Alexeiv's reserve battalions.

At 1530hrs on the 24th, Alexeiv evaluated the situation and decided to retreat. His mission was not to block the entire Japanese force, but rather to screen the routes leading to the rear of the 1st Manchurian Army. Alexeiv determined he could complete his task best by retreating some 10km, where the Chenghocheng Detachment would be roughly in line with the main Russian defences of Kuropatkin's armies, though still about 10km east of Linevich's 1st Army. At nightfall on the 24th, Alexeiv executed his retreat, thereby temporarily breaking contact with Kawamura's Yalu Army.

Besides Kawamura's Yalu Army, the 2nd Division of Kuroki's 1st Army was the only other Japanese unit to conduct offensive action up to 24 February. The 2nd Division advanced to a position on the extreme right of Kuroki's army, where it was ready to cooperate with the forthcoming further advance of Kawamura's army. The 2nd Division encountered some Siberian Cossacks in the course of the day's manoeuvre, which engaged it for about an hour before retiring. By the end of the 24th, Kuroki and Kawamura were positioned in accordance with Oyama's plans for action on the following day.

The staffs of both Linevich and Kuropatkin were well informed of all that had taken place from the 19th to the 24th. Linevich began to be concerned for the flank of his eastern corps, the 3rd Siberian Corps, and peeled off regiments from other corps to reinforce this flank. This was intensified when the Japanese 2nd Division conducted its manoeuvre on the 24th. Of much greater importance was the effect of Kawamura's attacks on Kuropatkin. By the night of the 24th, Kuropatkin, in conversation with Kaulbars, had determined to delay indefinitely the planned Russian offensive on the right – the renewed attack on San-de-pu. Kuropatkin's growing concern about Japanese attacks on his left, and the recognition that Nogi's 11th Division was located there, were enough to divert Kuropatkin's attention to the east. One of the determining factors behind this change was Kuropatkin's unwillingness to reinforce Kaulbars' 2nd Army with any of the General Reserve – for fear that he would soon need it in the east.

The Japanese were noted for dragging guns into position by hand when horses were not available or they could not otherwise access the position due to terrain or weather conditions. (Author's collection)

Ultimately, between 19 and 24 February, the Japanese plan had unfolded exactly as intended. Kawamura had advanced, pushing back the Chenghocheng Detachment, and Kuroki had wheeled his force into line with them. Meanwhile, the Russians had been induced to cancel their offensive in the west due to their fixation on Kawamura's force in the east.

The extent of their success was unknown to the Japanese at the time, though it is evident from deployments made by Kuropatkin on 25 February. That day, the Russian commander removed the 1st Siberian Corps from Kaulbars' command, and transferred it, along with two other brigades, to the rear of Linevich's 1st Manchurian Army. All of this took place before Linevich's main position had truly been engaged. In total, Kuropatkin dispatched 42 battalions and 128 cannon from Kaulbars' 2nd Army and his General Reserve to reinforce his left flank. Kuropatkin also redeployed, for the third time in just over a month, his best cavalryman, Rennenkampf. Rennenkampf would replace Alexeiv as commander of the Chenghocheng Detachment, again demonstrating Kuropatkin's total commitment to securing his left flank.

From 25–26 February, Nogi's Army remained concealed, while the Japanese 2nd and 4th Armies stayed in place, only skirmishing and conducting normal reconnaissance activities to their front. On the Japanese right, however, Kuroki's 1st Army and Kawamura's Yalu Army continued to manoeuvre and advance, resulting in further combat action in the east.

Beginning on the night of 24/25 February, Kuroki's Army began to intensify pressure on Linevich's 1st Manchurian Army, especially his 3rd Siberian Corps. Night attacks were made in many sections, with small but intense fights breaking out. In one sector, a battalion of the Japanese Guards Division (one of Kuroki's three divisions) attempted to storm a trench but was thrown back with 100 casualties, while in another sector, a several hundred-strong group of picked Russian infantrymen infiltrated Japanese lines and began to dismantle their obstacles until the Japanese defenders rushed to dispatch them with bayonets and hand grenades.

On the far right, Kawamura made little progress, his advance suffering from the ice and snow that continued to coat the steep slopes and narrow paths on which his men were advancing. Alexeiv still commanded the Chenghocheng Detachment, as Rennenkampf had not yet arrived (he had to travel some 70–80km to assume command). One further noteworthy event of the day was Oyama's decision to pull most of the Japanese 3rd Division from Oku's 2nd Army and move it to a position to support Nogi once he began his advance. Seemingly, Oyama understood the Russian threat to San-de-pu had subsided, allowing him to accept risk and begin massing the forces required for his main effort.

On the 26th, Kuroki's Guards Division and 12th Division attempted to push forward against Linevich's Army. However, after preliminary bombardments, the commanders demurred due to decreased visibility and terrible conditions from a snow and dust storm. To the right of these divisions, the 2nd Division began attacking Linevich's eastern positions in an attempt to turn his flank. While the Japanese regiments had not yet been successful, their clear goal of turning Linevich's flank caused concern throughout the Russian chain of command. Linevich reinforced the 35th East Siberian Regiment with eight squadrons of Cossacks to stabilize the situation. Heavy snow aided their efforts and began to severely impede the Japanese in this sector. As the day's events ended, one of the brigades dispatched by

Overview of the battle, 26–27 February 1905

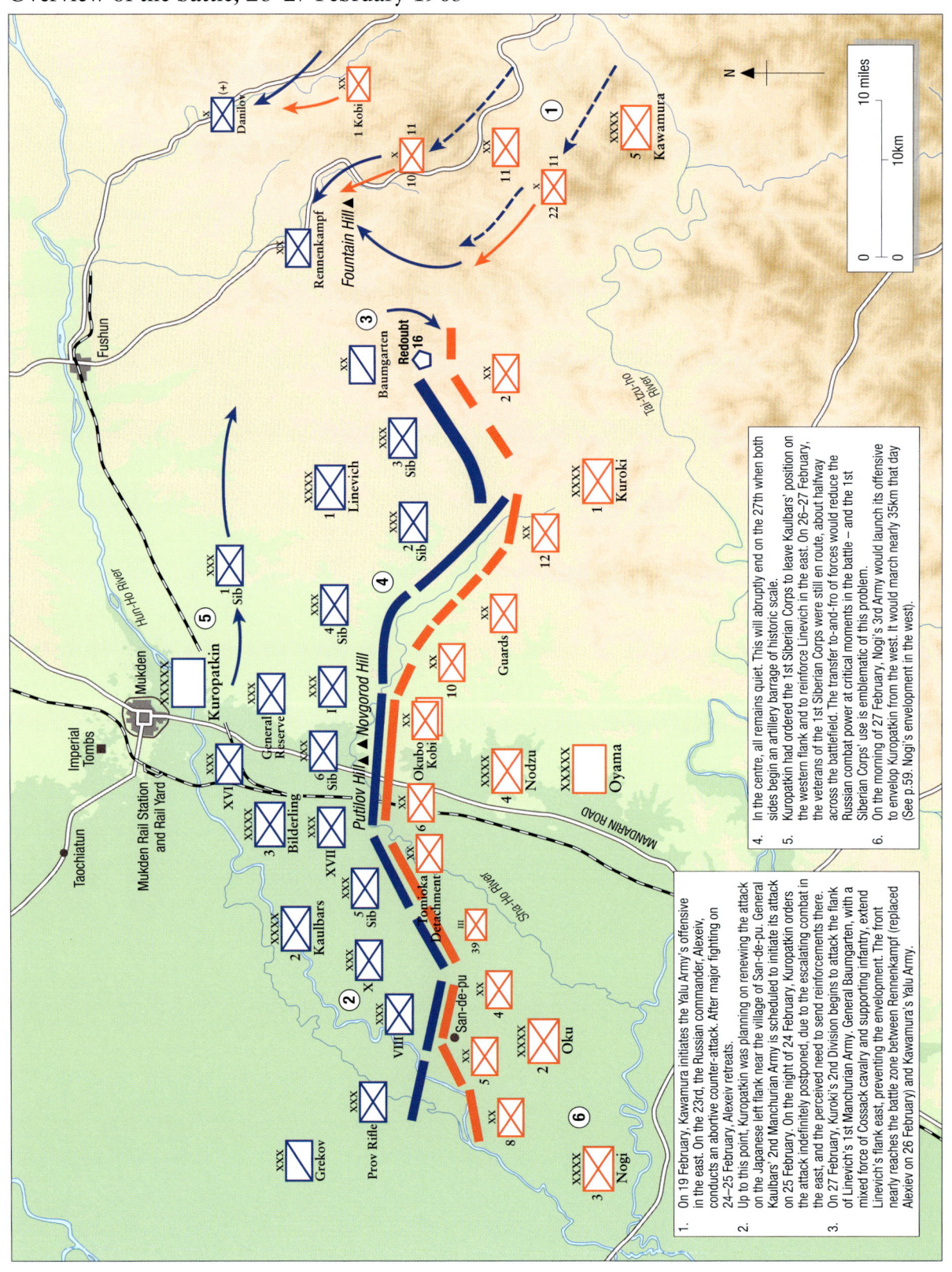

Kuropatkin from 2nd Army arrived in the rear area and became available to Linevich to extend his eastern flank still further. In short, 26 February saw Kuroki expanding the front line eastward, towards the combat developing between Kawamura and the Chenghocheng Detachment.

Kawamura pressed hard on Alexeiv on the far right, driving up two passes against the Russian screening forces. Due to some confusion, one of the subordinate commanders prematurely withdrew from his position, putting the rest of the detachment in peril of being cut off by the advancing Japanese. Alexeiv ordered a general retreat shortly before Rennenkampf arrived to take command of the detachment. Upon evaluating the situation, Rennenkampf decided to consolidate his force at Tu-pin-tai, about 7–10km north of the detachment's positions at the start of the day. Here he consolidated and improved his defences, incorporating reinforcements sent by Linevich the previous day.

As 26 February ended, fighting in the battle of Mukden was still constrained to the eastern third of the battlefield, while the centre and western flanks remained quiet. On the Japanese side, Kawamura's Yalu Army had initiated the offensive and advanced dozens of kilometres against the Russian flank guard, the Chenghocheng Detachment. Further to the west, Kuroki's 1st Army had begun attacking Linevich to position itself to further support Kawamura and put pressure on Linevich's flank. Rennenkampf's arrival meant that the Russians had a competent leader who had selected a strong position to consolidate his detachment and prepare for renewed combat on 27 February. Until 26 February, the Japanese had attacked with only Kawamura's Yalu Army, and to a lesser extent with Kuroki's 1st Army, perhaps 60,000–80,000 men in total. Out of Kuropatkin's force, only the Chenghocheng Detachment and Linevich's army had seen real combat. On the next day, 27 February, fighting would expand across the whole front of the armies – widening into the largest pitched battle in history.

PHASE II – INITIATION, 27–28 FEBRUARY

The eastern flank
During the night of 26/27 February, Rennenkampf benefited from Kuropatkin's transfer of reserves to the eastern flank. That night, Gen Danilov, leading a mixed force of reinforcements of about brigade strength, arrived on the flank and quickly took up a position to the east of Rennenkampf and under his overall command. By late morning on the 27th, Kawamura's Kobi Division collided with Danilov's force, while the 11th Japanese Division began its attack on the Russian forces directly under Rennenkampf – which were positioned around Fountain Hill. The fight between Danilov and the Kobi Division was not quite desperate that day, as the Japanese Division was slow to deploy its guns. The lines of Kobi infantry, attacking in open order, advanced no closer than 500m before withdrawing. That night, the Kobi Division made a stronger attack, Danilov ordering his force to fall back to elevated terrain to his rear. Rennenkampf's force, now consisting of approximately 16 battalions, ten squadrons and 26 guns, was even less intensely attacked, and the fighting to his front consisted mainly of both sides manoeuvring their guns into advantageous positions to shell their enemy's positions.

RUSSIAN
1. Two companies of 1st Battalion, 284th (Chembar) Regiment, with at least one machine gun
2. Two companies of 1st Battalion, 4th (Verkhne-Udinsk) Regiment, with at least one machine gun
3. Russian artillery fire from adjacent units
4. Russian artillery fire from Redoubt 18

Note: gridlines are shown at intervals of 500m (546.81 yards).

1 ⊠ 284 (Chembar) (-)

1 ⊠ 4 (Verkhane Udinsk) (-)

▼ EVENTS

1. Part of the Japanese 2nd Division advance through the Wang-fu-ling pass on the evening of the 26th, and receive orders for the next day. A Japanese machine gun battery is present to support maneuver of the 4th Regiment the following day.

2. In the early hours of 27 February, the two battalions move to their assault positions: 1st Battalion to the west, 3rd Battalion to the east. Sixty volunteers (30 from each battalion) were identified to breach the wire obstacles in front of Redoubt 16. Of these men, 42 of them are equipped with hand grenades and the other 18 with wire cutters. Here they wait until 0400hrs, despite intense cold.

3. The movement is slow due to the cold and ice from the snowstorm the previous day. The Russians open fire at 0550hrs. The volunteers begin cutting through the wire despite heavy casualties. Russian artillery fire from neighboring units (displayed here as swooping blue arrows) compounds the difficulties faced by the Japanese companies.

4. 0700hrs: Japanese mountain guns open up, but cause friendly casualties and have to adjust fire. A Japanese machine gun battery (F) also supports the maneuver of the infantry towards the redoubts.

5. One company of the 3rd Battalion take fire from a separate redoubt, Redoubt 17. This unit is pinned down and remains in place, engaging Redoubt 17 with rifle fire.

6. 0745hrs: The remaining attacking companies enter the breaches in the wire and storm the redoubt. By 0800hrs the redoubt is seized. Around 200 of the attacking Japanese and 100 Russians lay dead and wounded around this one redoubt.

THE STORMING OF REDOUBT 16, 27 FEBRUARY 1905

Since 25 February, Kuroki's Kobi brigade and 2nd Division have manoeuvred eastward in attempt to flank Linevich's III Siberian Corps. On 27 February, the 1st and 3rd Battalions of the 4th Regiment storm a redoubt located on high ground to their north in the morning. Unbeknownst to the Japanese 4th Regiment, this redoubt (16) is part of an extension of the Russian front that General Baumgarten's force is in the process of strengthening. This extension consisted of eight redoubts, beginning with Redoubt 16 and extending towards Rennenkampf's positions further in the east.

JAPANESE
A. 1st, 2nd and 3rd Companies, 1st Battalion, 4th Infantry Regiment
B. 10th Company, 3rd Battalion, 4th Infantry Regiment
C. 9th Company, 3rd Battalion, 4th Infantry Regiment
D. 12th Company, 3rd Battalion, 4th Infantry Regiment
E. Battery B, 2nd Artillery Regiment (six guns)
F. Japanese Machine Gun Battery

At this point, Rennemkampf's force, together with Danilov to the east, were positioned with their backs to the Hun-Ho River line, and had seemingly blocked the advance of Kawamura's Yalu Army. The Yalu Army would make very little forward progress in the coming days, though it was already in advance of, but far to the east of, Kuroki's army.

It is worth noting that in the early hours of 27 February, the temperature dropped to −8 degrees Fahrenheit, the coldest period of the entire battle. During these hours, the Japanese 2nd Division, Kuroki's furthest east and closest unit to the Yalu Army, attempted to wheel left and turn the flank of Linevich's 1st Manchurian Army. The intent of the Japanese was to exploit a perceived gap between Rennenkampf's detachment and the 1st Manchurian Army. Fortunately for the Russians, Linevich had positioned his cavalry division under Baumgarten in this area, extending his lines many kilometres further towards Rennenkampf's positions than the Japanese anticipated. The Japanese 2nd Division, therefore, made little progress as it advanced and continuously encountered Baumgarten's dismounted Cossacks with supporting infantry battalions and artillery.

The westernmost elements of the Japanese 2nd Division did have some success to their immediate front in seizing Redoubt 16, the first in a series of redoubts that anchored 3rd Siberian Corps' position. In the early hours of 27 February, 60 volunteer Japanese infantrymen lay in wait with wire cutters and hand grenades until 0430hrs, when the order to attack was given. While waiting, several of these men died from the intense cold, offering sobering testament to the dedication and resilience of the Japanese infantrymen in this battle. Behind theses volunteers were two battalions of the 4th Regiment, ready to exploit the breach in the wire that the selected men were tasked with creating. Defending the redoubt were only two companies of Russian infantry, though they were supported by at least one machine gun, which they soon put to devastating effect. As the loose lines of the Japanese infantry battalions rushed directly towards the redoubt, the volunteers had already begun to cut through the wire. The Russian machine gun opened fire, and within seconds had killed a Japanese captain and 50 of his soldiers. Nonetheless, the Japanese pressed the attack and, using hand grenades and suppressive fire from supporting light artillery, were able to constrain the defenders. Finally, pushing through the openings in the wire, the Japanese companies entered the redoubt, seizing it by 0800hrs. Two hundred Japanese, including more than half the volunteers, were killed or wounded in this operation, as well as 100 of the defending Russians. The intensity of the fighting for this one redoubt in a vast network of fortifications and trenches is revealing; there would be countless more fights like that at Redoubt 16 in the coming days.

Across the rest of the front of 1st Manchurian Army, the Japanese 12th and Guards Division made only ineffectual attacks. In the sector of the Japanese Guards Division, a persistent Russian artillery bombardment made any movement, let alone attacks, extremely hazardous. In the meantime, a further brigade of reinforcements, previously dispatched by Kuropatkin from the reserves, arrived at Linevich's position. At this point, Linevich accurately assessed that the strength of his force had grown superior to the Japanese to his front, and began to suggest to Kuropatkin, via telegraph, that the conditions might be favourable for him to attack and turn the flank of Kuroki's 1st Army. Kuropatkin was initially open to the suggestion, but did not give any definitive orders or direction to act on it.

Photographed at around the time of the battle, this image captures the nature of the terrain near Fountain Hill. (Author's collection)

On 28 February, the Japanese high command's focus shifted firmly to other parts of the battlefield. However, Kawamura's Kobi and 11th Divisions continued to relentlessly apply pressure to Rennenkampf and Danilov's sector. On the 28th, the Japanese attacks against Rennenkampf's force would be the fiercest of the whole battlefront. About 8 miles of severely restrictive, hilly terrain separated Rennenkampf's force from that of Danilov, but both formations continued to occupy blocking positions overlooking the most easily traversable routes through the hills. Danilov would continue to face the Kobi Division, while Rennenkampf would engage the 11th Division.

On the morning of the 28th, the Japanese began assaulting the forward position on Fountain Hill, held by Rennenkampf's Chernoyar infantry regiment. It had advantageously positioned two machine guns, which, from their points of elevation among the rolling hills, were able to place enfilade fire on the advancing Japanese. The Japanese, however, quickly manoeuvred their own machine guns onto similar terrain, driving the Russians from their positions with effective fire. The Japanese continued to attack the regiment once it established itself in a new position, but soon suffered terrible losses as they advanced within 100 yards of these Russian lines. The assault ceased only when a repositioned Russian machine gun and artillery from a neighbouring position opened fire. Thereafter, the Chernoyar Regiment soon reoccupied its original position on Fountain Hill.

At Danilov's position, the Japanese elected to avoid conducting a frontal attack, instead sending a battalion of infantry to envelop Danilov through the heights to his east. Danilov sent his own infantry to meet them on the top of the hill, resulting in bloody close-quarters fighting. Each of the Russian regiments engaged in the fighting lost several hundred men to secure Danilov's flank. Though Danilov successfully defended his position, Kuropatkin dispatched the Viborg Regiment from his General Reserve to further reinforce him. In doing this, Kuropatkin demonstrated his misunderstanding of the real threats to his armies' positions, which were then developing on his right flank.

West of Rennenkampf's fights with the Yalu Army, Linevich's force mostly engaged in an artillery duel with the 12th and Guards Divisions of Kuroki's 1st Army. At one point, the Russians massed 36 guns to conduct an artillery attack on the recently captured Redoubt 16, which brought more misery for the Japanese occupants, who were still suffering from the severe cold. They did have one stroke of luck when the Russians decided to call off their planned counter-attack on the redoubt.

JAPANESE 11IN (28CM) SIEGE ARTILLERY BATTERY IN ACTION, 1100HRS ON 28 FEBRUARY 1905 (PP.54–55)

On 28 February, the fighting which had mostly transpired on the eastern front expanded across the whole battlefront. In the centre, where fortifications, trenches and obstacles were densest, the day's fighting consisted of a massive artillery bombardment and duel. Beginning at about 1100hrs, the Japanese began to target Russian strong points and suspected troop concentrations, while the Russians replied, attempting to neutralize the Japanese artillery batteries. The scale of this bombardment marked a terrible and significant milestone in the history of warfare. Never had so many heavy guns been employed in a field engagement – in total, there were 200 heavy siege guns engaged on 28 February. The Japanese used their six 28cm howitzers to target forward concentrations of Russian troops, while the 15cm mortars and 12cm howitzers focused their fire on the Russian fortifications on Putilov and Novgorod hills. Lighter field guns joined in across the front, as the Russian heavy artillery responded, trying to locate and destroy the Japanese siege guns. Unlike at Port Arthur, where the terrain allowed for excellent protection, the Japanese artillery at Mukden was relatively exposed, relying on slight rises in elevation for concealment, and positions fortified with sandbags for cover.

The Japanese may have overestimated the effect of their targeting based on some Russian successes – in one case, a single Russian 5.9in shell stuck a troop shelter in the Japanese lines, killing 16 men in one strike. Despite the marginal direct impact of the artillery bombardment, the intensity (and noise) of Japanese firepower on 28 February did cause Kuropatkin to consider whether the Japanese main effort might occur in the centre after all – further complicating his understanding of the developing envelopment in the west.

Here a battery of two, 11in (28cm) howitzers are engaging Russian targets in the distance. The crews of one howitzer are retrieving ammunition and reloading it (**1**), while the other howitzer is firing (**2**). Behind the guns themselves is a 'crow's nest.' (**3**) This is a makeshift Japanese observation tower that allows an artillery officer to 'spot' for the battery. The officer in the tower is exposed to Russian observation, and artillery strikes are falling around the 'crow's nest.' One 'spotting' officer has already been wounded and is being treated prior to evacuation to an aid station (**4**). Russian artillery is exploding all throughout the distance on and above various suspected Japanese positions.

Battery of Japanese 11in howitzers in action at Mukden. This battery was located a few kilometres to the south-west of Putilov Hill. (Author's collection)

Bombardment in the centre

In the centre of the battlefield, the Russian and Japanese positions roughly paralleled the Sha-Ho River, with the Russians to the north and the Japanese to the south. This was not true around Putilov Hill and Novgorod Hill, which the Russians had occupied since the Sha-Ho battle. These hills stood out conspicuously, anchoring a Russian salient south of the Sha-Ho River. As stated previously, Bilderling's 3rd Manchurian Army was concentrated on a narrower front than any other, with its three corps occupying no more than an 18km sector. I Corps occupied the portion south of the Sha-Ho, encompassing the two hills, while the 4th Siberian Corps had elements north and south of the river, and the XVII Corps was wholly north of the river. Facing this formidable disposition of forces was Nodzu's 4th Japanese Army, consisting of two regular divisions, with a Kobi division in the centre. Nodzu himself retained three Kobi regiments as the 4th Army reserve.

For all these reasons, it is not surprising that the Japanese did not attempt to make direct attacks in this sector. Nodzu did, however, intend to carry out his mission of fixing the Russian centre in place. To accomplish this task, Nodzu's army possessed 108 pieces of heavy artillery. Many of these cannon had been recently transferred from the siege of Port Arthur, and they included the 28cm/11in howitzers, which would soon have the distinction of being the heaviest artillery ever employed in a field battle up to that point. On the 27th, this artillery opened up. The Japanese were attempting to weaken the Russian positions around Putilov Hill, while the Russians returned fire in an attempt to knock out the Japanese batteries. The crescendo increased the next day when witnesses described a notably louder rumble coming from the centre, audible some 30 miles away. One Russian heavy artillery shell penetrated a Japanese bunker, killing 16 soldiers. Through a macabre logic, the Japanese officers drew from this misfortune the conclusion that their artillery must be having considerable effect on the Russians, which was not quite the case. During the whole day, the Russian I Corps suffered only 33 casualties, despite being the focus of Japanese artillery efforts. This

A battery of 76.2mm M1900 guns fire, a common sight in late February 1905. (Photo by Photo12/Universal Images Group via Getty Images)

testifies to the extent, depth and quality of Russian fortification systems in this portion of the field.

Initiation of Nogi's 3rd Army on the western flank

On 27 February, Oyama was sufficiently satisfied with his assessment of Kuropatkin's prioritization of the east that he ordered Nogi to begin his advance in the west. Up to this point, Nogi's entire army was located some 10km to the rear of Oku's 2nd Army, where it was screened from observation and well-positioned to begin a wide envelopment of the Russian right.

Oku conducted some minor infantry probes along his lines in the early morning of the 27th, which coincided with Nogi's force beginning its advance. Nogi's army would essentially conduct a wide wheel, with the furthest right of his formations moving the shortest distance before attacking the flank units of the Russian 2nd Manchurian Army, while each subsequent unit would have a longer, wider wheeling route before turning east and enveloping the Russians. Moving from inner wheel to outer, Nogi's forces were arranged in the following manner: the 9th Division in inner wheel, then the 7th Division, 15th Kobi Brigade, 1st Division on the outer left and the 2nd Cavalry Brigade being their flank guard, furthest on the left.

On the 27th, Nogi made rapid progress, with the inner 9th Division marching 10km and the outer 1st Division and cavalry moving nearly 20km to Kao-li-ma. Barely a shot was fired on this day, as the Russian cavalry units in Nogi's path, primarily the 4th and 5th Ural Cossacks, continuously fell back in the face of the Japanese advance, maintaining a distance for observation only. These Cossack units did observe enough to realize a major attack was underway, and reports made their way to Kaulbars, though they were not yet clear on position and number of Japanese units involved. Kaulbars' first action was to order the cavalry commander, Gen Grekov, to extend his flank and continue observing.

On 28 February, the Japanese made still further progress. This day, Grekov did determine to use his cavalry to delay the Japanese advance, though his effort was botched. He continuously divided what regiments he had, which did not perform well in their assigned missions. One such action was that of the 5th Ural Cossacks and one battery of Cossack horse artillery, who did succeed in deploying upon seeing the 1st Japanese Division marching on the far right. When the Cossack artillery opened fire, the 1st Division did not even stop its march, but merely deployed one battalion to chase away the force. In total, the Russian cavalry on the flank suffered fewer than 20 casualties on the 28th – which attests to their less-than-vigorous efforts that day.

Japanese infantry on the march. Nogi's 'wheel' to envelop the Russian flank would have looked like this on 27 and 28 February 1905. (Author's collection)

At this point, Kaulbars and Kuropatkin knew that the Japanese 3rd Army posed severe danger to the Russian right flank. However, Russian reporting on the position of Nogi's units seems to have been consistently 'behind', stating that the Japanese were at one village, when they had already advanced several more kilometres. Kaulbars began to pull several regiments from his front

Nogi's envelopment in the west, 27 February to 1 March 1905

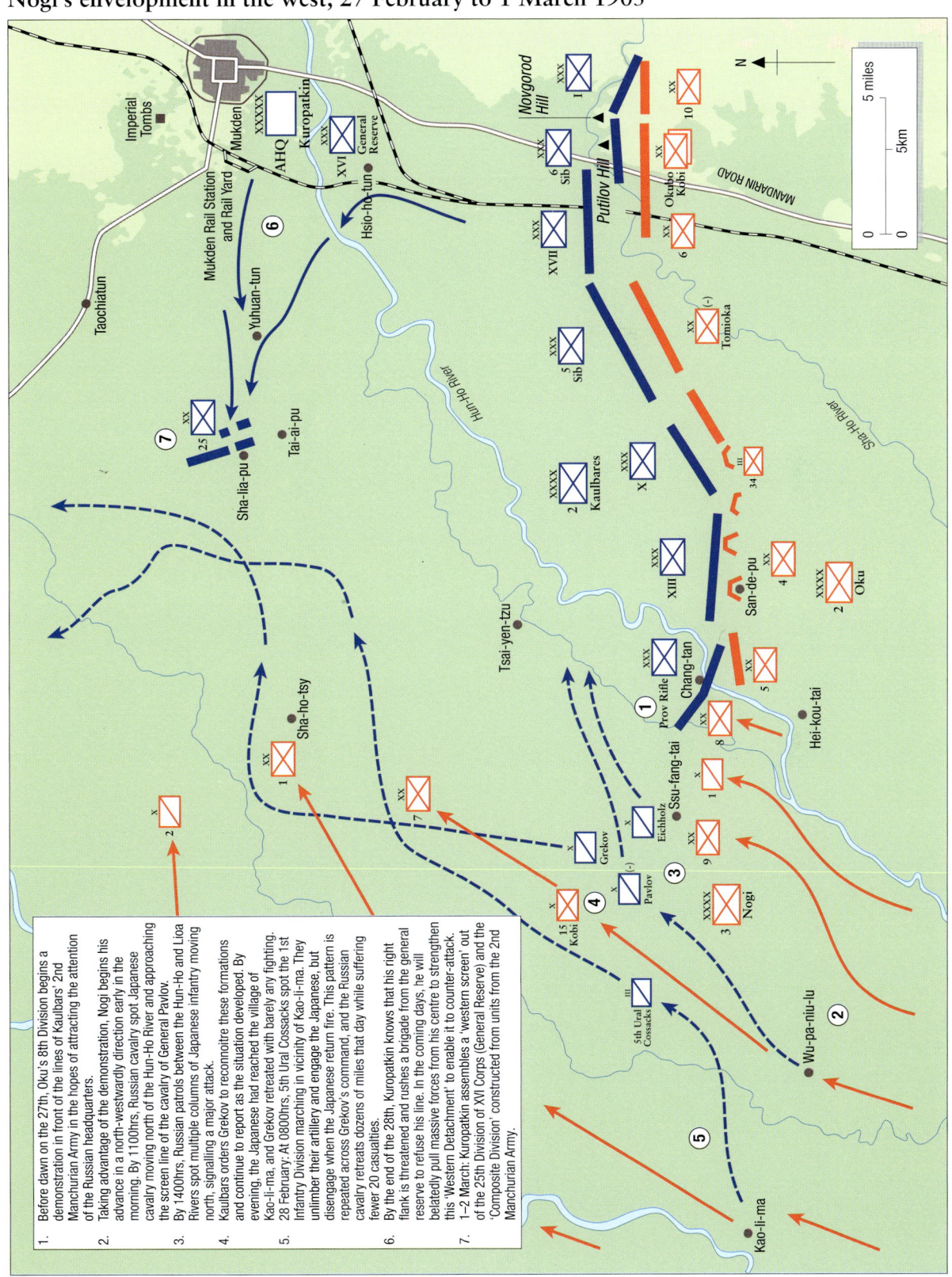

5TH URAL COSSACKS SIGHT JAPANESE 1ST INFANTRY DIVISION, 0800HRS ON 28 FEBRUARY 1905 (PP.60–61)

On 27 February, General Nogi's 3rd Japanese Army began its wide enveloping manoeuvre in the far west of the battlefield. The Ural Cossacks of Grekov's force spotted the Japanese columns moving that day, and Kaulbars was soon made aware of the reports of Japanese activity. Kaulbars immediately ordered Grekov to extend his screening line further west, and to actively reconnoiter the entire region through which the Japanese columns were moving. During the night of the 27/28, only scattered shots of pickets and patrols were heard, as the Japanese and Russians alike elected to bivouac for the night. The next morning Grekov ordered the 5th Ural Cossacks, with an attached battery of the 1st Trans-Baikal Cossack Battery, to reconnoiter the area around the village of Kao-li-ma, where patrols identified the marching column of the Japanese 1st Infantry Division moving rapidly north.

Here, (**1**) the Japanese 1st Infantry Division marches towards the village of Kao-li-ma. They are using a road march formation to maximize their speed, which was considerable (up to 20km per day). Each regiment deployed a company or so into skirmish formation to provide some security for the advance (**2**). They are marching past a walled village (**3**), one of the myriad settlements that populated the countryside. Observers of the war frequently commented on the dense population of the region. At Kao-li-ma (**4**), another walled village, a patrol of Cossacks estimates the strength of the Japanese before remounting and withdrawing (**5**). To avoid detection, one Cossack holds the horses of three others (**6**) to allow them to move to the edge of the village and observe the Japanese with binoculars.

When the Ural Cossacks deployed two squadrons and began firing at the columns, the Japanese did not halt, but simply deployed a single battalion into open order to clear the area from which the artillery was firing. Before long, a battery of Japanese artillery joined the engagement, at which point the 5th Ural Cossacks disengaged. They did not suffer a casualty in this encounter. The 5th Ural Cossacks reconnaissance at Kao-li-ma was emblematic of Grekov's cavalry corps' efforts from 27 February to 1 March. They were in the right place, and properly postured to disrupt or at least delay the Japanese advance. Instead, through an aversion to casualties or a lack of clear leadership from the regimental level up, the Russian cavalry under Grekov failed in every respect to serve as the flanks screen, let alone guard, of Kuropatkin's armies.

line and position them as an army reserve, though he did not act decisively to support the cavalry on the far right. Kuropatkin, upon hearing of the developing situation on the far right, dispatched a brigade from the General Reserve to positions west of Mukden. Evidence of Kuropatkin's confusion and growing anxiety was his simultaneous dispatch of yet another regiment to the eastern flank. In essence, while Kuropatkin was aware at this point that the attack on his right was a serious threat, he was not yet ready to accept risk anywhere else on the battlefield to address the emerging envelopment.

PHASE III – ENVELOPMENT, 1–3 MARCH

Nogi
On the outside of Nogi's wheel movement, where the Japanese 2nd Cavalry Brigade and 1st Infantry Division were marching, the envelopment proceeded nearly unimpeded. The 1st Infantry Division marched some 24km on 1 March before stopping to bivouac for the night, and the Cavalry Brigade on its flank even further. When the cavalry stopped its movement for the day, it was at a position 15km due north-east of Mukden. The Russians did manage to rush reinforcements to this sector of the battlefield. This was the 2nd Brigade of the 41st Division, which Kuropatkin dispatched from the General Reserve the previous day. The brigade was commanded by Gen Birger and marched nearly 60km in 24 hours to join the 4th Ural Cossack Regiment on the furthest right flank of the Russian armies, by this time located north-east of the city of Mukden. Birger and the Ural Cossacks were now positioned to dispute the advance of the cavalry and 1st Division on 2 March.

Nogi's inner wheel, consisting of the 7th and 9th Divisions, was by this time running into units of Kaulbars' 2nd Manchurian Army. Consequentially, their forward progress was not as rapid. In the innermost section of the wheel, the Japanese 9th Division, now supported by the 1st Cavalry Brigade (sent over from Oku's Army), began a morning assault on the village of Ssu-fang-tai, which was on an elevation overlooking the surrounding plain. It was therefore a great defensive point for the Russians, who included a mixed force of the retreating cavalry of Grekov and eight battalions of Kaulbars' right-flank Rifle Corps. The Japanese assault battalions were effectively engaged by rifle fire and field artillery, which was very effective due to the excellent observation available from the village. The assault was thrown back all day, and only succeeded at 2000hrs. At that point, Kaulbars ordered a retreat due to the Japanese 2nd Cavalry Brigade and 1st Infantry Division's operational-level envelopment to the north. The Japanese 9th Division and 1st Cavalry Brigade lost 700 men on 1 March, demonstrating that with

Oku's 41st Regiment of the 5th Division in combat on 2 March. These troops formed the hinge between Nogi and Oku and fought fiercely. (Author's collection)

APRÈS LA BATAILLE DE MOUKDEN

This contemporary illustration captures the severity of winter conditions that existed through much of the battle. (Photo by DEA/G. DAGLI ORTI/De Agostini via Getty Images)

competent and wilful leadership, Russian units could delay or even halt the Japanese enveloping units.

Gen Kaulbars' 2nd Manchurian Army continued to face Oku's 2nd Army to the south. Oku was given orders to attack on 1 March, to add to Kaulbars and 2nd Manchurian Army's troubles. Oku therefore ordered his 8th and 5th Divisions to attack multiple villages in front of their positions. The two villages in front of the 8th Division were held by no more than two Russian battalions each. However, in this somewhat constrained and static sector of the front, the Russians were able to leverage their superior strength in artillery, and while the 8th Division seized its objectives, they suffered heavily from Russian artillery and the villages they captured were reduced to smouldering ruins by Russian guns by the end of the day.

The 5th Division's attacks initially made some headway. The ground over which the Japanese attacked here was especially flat and open, and the Japanese moved in waves of unusually dispersed infantrymen (5–6m between each soldier). The Russians apparently had trouble engaging this formation with their rifle and artillery fire. This advantage was soon neutralized, however, when the Russians engaged the Japanese infantry with four machine guns. The carnage from enfilade fire was extreme, and was only brought to a halt when volunteer Japanese infantrymen rolled the small mountain cannons to within 500 yards of the machine-gun positions and destroyed two of them, causing the other two to withdraw. The 11th Regiment alone (one of four in the division) lost 1,000 men in this assault.

Kuropatkin at this point is thought to have acknowledged that Nogi's long-feared 3rd Army was the force enveloping his right. He therefore began to strip units from the corps of Kaulbars and Bilderling, which were still facing Japanese armies to the south, in order to create a new line facing west against Nogi. Building on the brigade of Birger, which was already north-east of Mukden, Kuropatkin pulled a division of 16 battalions from the XVI Corps of the General Reserve and from Kaulbars' 2nd Army. He then ordered Kaulbars to provide 32 further battalions as the situation developed. While it was reasonable for Kuropatkin to act decisively to refuse his line and parry Nogi's attack, the Russian commander was increasingly mixing units to the point that they would soon have no integrity above the regimental level. Commanders and staffs were constantly transferring, receiving, establishing communications with and integrating units they had never before commanded. Meanwhile, this element was almost completely absent in the Japanese armies, which, even ten days into the battle, were essentially still in their original task organization and executing their original plan.

On 2 March, Kuropatkin continued to oversee the assembly of this western-facing force about 15km west of the city of Mukden. Birger's detachment formed the northern flank, but was not attacked on 2 March.

To the south of Birger, however, Kuropatkin's element would begin to contest Nogi's advance. The 25th Division from the General Reserve (Topornin's corps) and the 'Composite Division' from 2nd Manchurian Army were directed to form the centre of Kuropatkin's westward-facing line, and collided with Nogi's force near the village of Sha-lin-pu. Meanwhile, the 1st Siberian Corps was still moving from the eastern flank in accordance with Kuropatkin's orders, but would require a day or two more to be in position. Kaulbars would spend 2 March pulling together the additional two divisions of troops from his line that he was required to send to Kuropatkin.

PENDANT LA BATAILLE
L'envoyé spécial du Petit Journal en Mandchourie suit les péripéties du combat

Perhaps somewhat stylized, this image nonetheless portrays a common scene in the heavily populated but otherwise open landscape south of Mukden. (Photo by Roger Viollet Collection/Getty Images)

While Kuropatkin's new force would still be concentrating through the night of 3 March, its first divisions would already begin fighting on the 2nd. Approximately a brigade each from the 'Composite Division' and the 25th Division converged from three directions to attack the village of Sha-lin-pu. The brigade from the 'Composite Division' commanded by Gen Shatilov attacked Sha-lin-pu directly, which had just been occupied by the Japanese 7th Division. Shatilov was outmatched as he did not have any artillery with him, and the Japanese kept up withering rifle fire. Meanwhile, a brigade from the 25th Division was manoeuvring to attack Sha-lin-pu from the north-east when it encountered elements of the Japanese 1st Division, which it fought for the entirety of the day. While the Russians failed to defeat the Japanese divisions or seize any terrain, the fighting on 2 March was bloody, with one Japanese brigade suffering 600 casualties and Nogi electing to commit a reserve Kobi brigade to the fight to stabilize his lines.

In addition to the fight at Sha-lin-pu, further south Nogi's 9th Division received an even sharper counter-attack. By this point, Kaulbars had successfully assembled 16 of the 32 battalions required by Kuropatkin for the new westward-facing line. This force, commanded by Gen Golembatovski, began engaging Nogi's 9th Division by attacking two different villages, each with two infantry regiments. Both of these attacks were successful, and the one by the Buzuluk and Minsk Regiments against the village of Tsai-yen-tzu resulted in the capture of seven Japanese machine guns and 64 prisoners. These regiments were then ordered to retreat to the main Russian lines, but their bold attack temporarily stunned the Japanese.

Meanwhile, Kaulbars was preparing to take command of the 'western screen' – the force being assembled by Kuropatkin. After giving orders to his 2nd Manchurian Army to reconsolidate, he handed over command to Gen von der Launitz. While von der Launitz was attempting to take command of his army, Oku's 2nd Army made an advance across its front, pushing back the now much-diminished 2nd Manchurian Army. The units of X Corps fell back approximately 10km in the face of the Japanese advance, to where they would eventually assume a roughly westward-facing line that connected

Excellent perspective of the Russian Irkutsk Regiment at the battle of Mukden. The uniforms of average Russian soldiers and the nature of the landscape are clearly captured. (Sueddeutsche Zeitung Photo/Alamy Stock Photo)

with Kaulbars' 'western screen', and formed a right angle with Bilderling's still southern-facing 3rd Manchurian Army in the centre. Bilderling received an order from Kuropatkin to provide four more regiments to assist on the western flank. For unknown reasons, he provided the equivalent of five regiments, which would be commanded by Gen De Witt and would soon become another formation joining the 'western screen'.

On 3 March, Nogi held his advancing army in place, to allow his 9th Division, which had fallen behind the other units, to resume its place in Nogi's turning wheel. On the far left of Nogi's position, the 2nd Cavalry Brigade nearly cut off Birger's mixed infantry and cavalry force. After fighting a day-long battle, Birger retreated north-east.

Elsewhere, Nogi's forces' only fighting was due to Russian counter-attacks. The 25th Division under Topornin and Shatilov renewed its attacks against the Japanese 7th and 1st Divisions around Sha-lin-pu. After some heavy fighting, Topornin's northern flank regiment was caught in enfilade fire, leading to some panic in the Russian higher command. Eventually, Kaulbars ordered Topornin's 25th Division and the 'Composite Division' to retreat some 5km east towards Mukden where they formed a new line.

Meanwhile, von der Launitz and the remaining formations of 2nd Manchurian Army were retreating and being pursued by Oku's 2nd Army. They were converging on the new line being formed by Kaulbars and the other retreating units, west and south-west of Mukden. By the night of 3 March, the Russian right flank was located some 10km west of Mukden, facing west and running to the south-west of Mukden, eventually connecting with Bilderling's force in the centre, which essentially remained in place.

At 1515hrs, Gen Kuropatkin made two decisions and relayed them in a memorandum to his commanders. First, he was personally moving his headquarters to Mukden. Second, once the 2nd Manchurian Army had completed its retreat and reconsolidated south-west and west of Mukden, he would prepare it and other units for a concerted counter-attack to be conducted on 4 or 5 March. Kuropatkin was formulating a plan to regain the initiative and save the battle by defeating Nogi's enveloping 3rd Army.

The centre and the east

While Nogi's envelopment was unfolding in the west, things were much more static in the centre and east, though equally bloody. Nodzu's 4th Army heavily bombarded Russian defensive and artillery positions throughout the day of 1 March. While these were the most heavily defended portion of the Russian line, that did not prevent Nodzu from conducting night attacks on

Another contemporary photograph of Russian infantry at Mukden. (Author's collection)

various Russian positions in brigade strength, including around Putilov Hill – seemingly, merely to play a part in applying pressure across Kuropatkin's entire line. The result was tremendous hardship for the Japanese infantry. Once the 4th Army's brigades began their attack at nightfall on 1 March, they made some progress, advancing with sappers in the front to clear wire and other obstacles. The Japanese continued to work through the wire until daybreak, when they broke off the attack rather than be killed in the open by Russian rifle and artillery fire. On the 2nd, hearing about the success that Oku's Army was achieving turning the flank of the Russian 2nd Manchurian Army, Nodzu's 4th Army pushed the attack in the centre. In the face of severe casualties, the Japanese 10th Division seized the first line of trenches to its front. However, once occupying these trenches, it immediately began to take fire from surrounding redoubts and Putilov Hill; nonetheless, it remained in place through the coming days at immense cost.

Further to the east, Kuroki demurred from attacking the Russian centre on 1 March, realizing that it was too strong and intact to break through. Only his right flank attempted to seize Russian positions, attacking the next three redoubts in a series connected with the already captured Redoubt 16. On 1 March, the Japanese 2nd Division accomplished this task, capturing Redoubts 17, 18, 19, but also stretching itself thin both in disposition and due to casualties. This was notable, as Linevich had been pushing to conduct a Russian offensive against just this portion of his front. However, Kuropatkin had already initiated the transfer of the 1st Siberian Corps from Linevich to the new right wing of the Russian armies that was being thrown together. On 2 March, Kuroki's Guards, 12th and 2nd Divisions pushed all along the front. These units made only limited gains, despite intense fighting and heavy losses. Most notably, the 2nd Division captured two further redoubts, 20 and 23, which left hundreds of Russian and Japanese corpses strewn across these hills. Despite this heavy fighting, the Russian centre and left were holding firm.

On the far eastern flank, Kawamura did not relent in his efforts to drive Rennenkampf and Danilov from their blocking positions. The 11th Division conducted furious attacks at Fountain Hill, located on Rennenkampf's flank. The hill changed hands multiple times, testifying to the resilience of Rennenkampf's men, who were fighting over a hill with Nogi's Port Arthur veterans. At one point, Rennenkampf personally directed into the fight two battalions of the Drissa Regiment, his last reserves, stabilizing the front. At the end of the fighting, Rennenkampf's position held strong. Further to the east, Danilov fought a similarly desperate fight with the Kobi Division.

RENNENKAMPF GUIDING IN HIS LAST RESERVE ON FOUNTAIN HILL, 1400HRS ON 1 MARCH 1905 (PP.68–69)

General Rennenkampf arrived on the Eastern Flank to take over command of the Chenghocheng Detachment at around 1700hrs on 26 February and soon ordered his units to consolidate at a position south of Machuntan, based on the town of Tu-pin-tai and Wu-pa-niu-pu-tzu (dominated by Fountain Hill). By midnight of the 26/27, they were partially prepared to defend against the veteran 11th Division of Kawamura's Yalu (5th Army). The Fountain Hill position had been planned as a possible defensive position in weeks past, but due to a shortage of laborers in the area had not been fortified.

Fighting began on the 27th before any serious preparations could be made. On 28 February, the 282nd Chernoyar Regiment held Fountain Hill against the repeated attacks of the 22nd Brigade of the 11th Division, using its two machine guns to inflict severe losses on the Japanese. Later that day, the Japanese were able to position one of their own machine guns to deliver enfilade fire on the Chernoyar Regiment on the hilltop, inflicting serious casualties and allowing the Japanese to briefly seize the summit, until they were forced to withdraw by accurate Russian artillery.

By 1 March, the Chernoyar Regiment was defending the hill again. Here Japanese companies of the 22nd Brigade are advancing on the Fountain Hill position (**1**), but are still 1,000 yards out. The Japanese have a machine gun in a support by fire position, attempting to suppress the Russians defending the hill (**2**). The remnants of a company of the Chernoyar Regiment are defending the hill from behind a slight ridgeline, and have added some sandbags to improve their position, but have not been able to dig a trench in this position yet. A single Maxim machine gun (**3**) is in operation to their flank, adding much needed firepower to the hard-pressed Chernoyar. Casualties from this and previous days fighting are scattered around (**4**). To solidify the position in the face of renewed attack, Rennenkampf (**5**) has personally guided two battalions of the Drissa Regiment to the portion of the position they will occupy (**6**). The lead company of the Drissa Regiment is moving at the 'double quick' to occupy a defensive position along the ridge line.

The reinforcement provided enough strength to defeat the Japanese assault and solidify the defenses of Fountain Hill. The hill would change hands many more times in coming days, but Rennenkampf's position south of Machuntan would hold until they received orders to retreat from Kuropatkin on 7 March.

By the day's end, Rennenkampf's relatively small detachment had lost over 1,000 men, and Danilov's more than 500. The Japanese losses are not accurately known. The intensity of this fighting should be remembered in the context that Kawamura knew that his was a subsidiary effort. Nonetheless, the Japanese Yalu Army continued to attack as if the war depended on its victory. On 2 and 3 March, the battle for Fountain Hill was renewed, with the hill changing hands twice more, and at the end of both days, neither side held the summit. Danilov's detachment also fought off renewed assaults on the 2nd. However, on 3 March, Danilov's sector was so quiet that Rennenkampf recommended that he attack the Japanese to his front. Danilov made a less than spirited attack, which was quickly pushed back by machine-gun fire. Nonetheless, the actions of Rennenkampf and Danilov were enough to cause concern in the Japanese high command. Late on 3 March, Oyama ordered Kuroki to move his 2nd Division further to the east to begin assisting Kawamura on the flank.

PHASE IV – RUSSIAN COUNTER-ATTACK, 4–7 MARCH

Russian counter-attack on the Western Flank
The general disposition of the Russian armies was now that of a semicircle around the city of Mukden, with the southern portion extending straight east for some 50km (the lines of Linevich's 1st Manchurian Army and Rennenkampf's detachment). However, the most significant feature of the battlefield was the rail line, running north–south slightly west of the city of Mukden. In essence, the 'western screen', now commanded by Kaulbars, was fighting with its back increasingly approaching Kuropatkin's line of supply, communication and retreat. By 4 March, the 'western screen' was set in position less than 10km west of the rail line. Kuropatkin's line could hardly fall back any more in the west without imperilling the entire Russian force. In the south, however, it was possible to order the forces of Rennenkampf and Linevich, and much of those of Bilderling, to fall back. They were still holding the line of the Sha-Ho River, though behind them was another defensible line at the Hun-Ho. Kuropatkin did not order these armies to fall back yet, as they continued to hold fast despite relentless Japanese attacks. Ultimately, the battle was likely to be decided on the western flank, where Nogi's army was rapidly approaching the rail line protected by Kaulbars' 'western screen'.

Kuropatkin wished to begin his counter-attack against Nogi on 4 March, but after consultation with Kaulbars, was convinced to delay until the 5th. Many of the units for the 'western screen' were still being assembled, most notably the still uncommitted 1st Siberian Corps. The latter had been transferred from Kuropatkin's western flank to the eastern flank and back again, in the space of seven days, without being engaged. While this was partially good news, as it was still fresh on 4 March, its constant shuttling around the battlefield reflected Kuropatkin's confusion about Japanese intentions, and effectively reduced his combat power during a crucial period of the battle.

Oyama seemed not to have realized that the Russians had assembled such a large force on the western flank, protecting the rail line and Mukden,

Russians defending a village near Mukden. This scene repeated itself many times, especially along the lines of Kuropatkin's 'western screen'. (Photo by Roger Viollet Collection/Getty Images)

and preparing for a counter-attack. Kuropatkin would commit to launching a counter-attack of 50 battalions the next day, and his staff successfully issued orders in accordance with this plan. Oyama's orders to Nogi's army on 4 March reflected a misplaced sense of imminent victory. The objectives Nogi's divisions received for the 4th implied a belief that they would continue a nearly unimpeded march, brushing aside retreating Russian units, and enter Mukden itself. Instead, Nogi's force would soon run into reinforcing Russian brigades.

On 4 March, the Japanese 7th and 9th Divisions encountered multiple Russian brigades dug in some 10km west of Mukden. In both cases, the Japanese deployed to attack, but were met by heavy Russian artillery fire, which suppressed their own guns and made movement difficult for their infantry. The infantry attacks that followed were not fully committed, dissipating at a distance of 1,000 yards from the Russian lines. The Japanese also did not attack that night.

Further to the south, Oku's 2nd Army was pursuing what it still expected to be a broken army. In reality, while von der Launitz's 2nd Manchurian Army was very disorganized, it did have enough time to re-establish itself in a continuous defensive position connecting Kaulbars' screen to Bilderling's 3rd Manchurian Army. Oku wanted to pursue the 2nd Manchurian Army across his whole front, which would require his entire army to cross the Hun-Ho. He could not do this, however, unless Nodzu's 4th Army made additional headway against the Russian centre. Towards this end, Oyama approved Oku's suggestion to give his 4th Division to Nodzu in an effort to advance the Japanese centre.

As the 4th Division was being transferred to Nodzu, Oku's army was advancing through the old positions of the 2nd Manchurian Army, moving towards the refused line which joined the armies of Kaulbars and von der Launitz with that of Bilderling. The 5th and 8th Divisions were able to advance easily until they came up against the westward-facing lines of von der Launitz, where massed Russian artillery checked the Japanese. Further east, the 4th Division, now part of Nodzu's 4th Army, became heavily engaged with Bilderling's right flank, especially his 5th Siberian Cavalry. The fighting centred on the village of Lan-shan-pu, which the 4th Japanese Division successfully stormed shortly after 1300hrs. The Russian 5th Siberian Corps made three attempts to retake it. In the third attempt, the Russians assembled 16 battalions that slowly advanced at dusk towards the Japanese, who held their fire until the Russians were within 20 yards. When the Japanese opened fire, terrible carnage ensued, eventually forcing back the Russians. One of the Japanese 4th Division's two brigades, the 19th, lost 1,000 men in this action.

On 4 March, Oyama made the decision to commit the last of his general reserve. He dispatched the three Kobi brigades – the 1st, 13th and 14th – to join Nogi. Oyama believed that, in retrospect, Nogi's force had not been weighted strongly enough for the decisive task it was given. These three additional brigades would hopefully provide Nogi with the manpower necessary to finish his envelopment.

In his orders for 5 March, Kuropatkin demonstrated a failure to learn from his enemy's success, as he was only ordering Kaulbars to take the offensive that day, while Bilderling in the centre focused on refusing his line, and the left flank was merely ordered to hold fast. In contrast, whenever Oyama took the offensive, nearly all his armies attacked the enemy to their respective fronts, in order to gain and maintain the initiative.

Despite many technological marvels in the early 20th century, war was still a human endeavour, as well as one involving tens of thousands of horses. (Photo by Burton Holmes/Archive Farms/Getty Images)

Early in the morning, Kaulbars issued orders for the much-anticipated Russian counter-attack. Kaulbars now commanded the entire 'western screen' and the remnants of the 2nd Manchurian Army, as the repeated transfer and shuffling of units left von der Launitz without any remaining units. At this point, the Russians began to refer to Kaulbars' entire force collectively as the 2nd Manchurian Army. Kaulbars intensified the failing of Kuropatkin by limiting the actual counter-attack to only the right flank of his army, which consisted of the 50 battalions under Lt Gen Gerngross. Kaulbars' remaining 16 battalions under Topornin and 34 battalions under Tserpitski were to hold fast, only attacking once Gerngross' attack had developed and Nogi's left flank had begun to retreat. At this decisive moment of the battle, the equivalent of about half of one Manchurian Army would be taking the offensive. Kaulbars' orders were for Gerngross to initiate the assault at 0930hrs, which Gerngross received at 0500hrs. However, Gerngross inexplicably took five further hours to issue his own orders to his command. Even after issuing his orders, he began a long series of scouting actions and small movements across his front to prepare for his attack, which would not actually begin until late afternoon. This delay would result in additional ramifications across the front. In the end, only three of Gerngross' regiments (25 per cent of his force) advanced on the 5th, and only one, the Samara Regiment, seized any ground.

Opposite Kaulbars, Nogi had determined not to attack on the 5th. Instead, he was executing a difficult manoeuvre by which he would pull his right flank unit, the 9th Division, out of the line and transfer it to his centre. This would enable the 1st Division to extend the army's flank further north. This was somewhat risky, for at one point on 6 March, this would require the 1st Division to open up a portion of the front for the 9th Division to occupy. Nogi began executing this action in the late afternoon, which coincided with the arrival in his rear area, though still many kilometres from the front, of the three Kobi brigades, which had been dispatched by Oyama a day earlier. Nogi would soon be weighting his left flank by a division, at the expense of his right, and strengthening his left flank by three Kobi brigades. This was happening at the same time that the Russians' attention was moving south to where Oku was pressing a vicious attack.

On 5 March, Oku determined to attack the Russians to his front with his 5th and 8th Divisions. These were the units under Tserpitski – Kaulbars' left-flank commander. Tserpitski was prepared to defend that day, and his soldiers were entrenched in well-fortified positions overlooking a mostly flat, featureless plain. After some skirmishing around 0700hrs, an artillery duel began at 0800hrs, in which the Russian artillery generally came out on top. At 0930hrs, the time Gerngross was supposed to begin the Russian counter-attack, Oku's men went into action. The 8th Division attacked with initially five infantry battalions at three points across a 5-mile front. They took accurate artillery fire in the advance, and were forced to halt about 1,000 yards from the Russian lines. The infantry battalions essentially lay prone, returning fire while they waited for reinforcement. Infantry, field artillery and mountain guns were brought up to support the assault, but little headway had been made by 1600hrs and the 8th Division had already suffered 1,000 casualties. There was a further attack made in the early evening that made little further progress. To the north, Oku's 5th Division fared slightly better, but also struggled to make headway due to the superiority of the Russian artillery. Nonetheless, Tserpitski felt pressure from these two Japanese divisions, mistakenly reporting to Kaulbars that he was being attacked by three divisions. Had this been true, he still should have been able to calmly defend his position, as his force of 34 battalions was nearly equivalent to three Japanese divisions and he was defending an entrenched position. Nonetheless, Kuropatkin, who also heard the report, interpreted this concentration to signify an attempt by the Japanese to penetrate his front rather than envelop it. Consequently, Kaulbars took the initiative to dispatch a brigade from Gerngross' counter-attack force to reinforce Tserpitski. This transfer took place as Gerngross was finally beginning his assault – a most inopportune time. Tserpitski, despite his panicked and mistaken report, which had unfortunate consequences, held his position without issue. The Japanese 5th Division suffered even more than the 8th, losing 1,500 men on 5 March.

On 6 March, Kaulbars finally initiated a sizeable attack. Early in the morning, 160 guns of the 1st Siberian Corps and De Witt's division began firing at Japanese positions, which they suspected were the Japanese 1st Division – Nogi's left flank. In reality, Nogi had already extended his left flank some 6 or 7km further north, to make room for the 9th Division to occupy almost precisely the spot the Russians were attacking. At the time of the actual Russian attack around late morning, the Japanese had one battalion covering this portion of the line. Nogi, however, quickly accelerated the 9th Division's march to fill the line, in the meantime massing his own batteries of over 100 field and mountain guns which bombarded the attacking Russian regiments. In the end, Gerngross did not dedicate enough force to the attack, with only a few regiments pushing into the Japanese line before being driven back. These regiments, however, did conduct a spirited assault, and the fighting was costly for both Russian and Japanese units in this sector. On a larger scale, Kaulbars failed by still adhering to the idea of an attack in echelon, with Gerngross attacking while Topornin's battalions to the south only supported until progress was made. Meanwhile, Tserpitski continued to hold steady in the face of some Japanese assaults, but he still continuously called his higher headquarters requesting more reinforcements, despite this being unnecessary. From the Japanese perspective, Tserpitski's position was very problematic, as their batteries repeatedly failed to locate the Russian artillery, which was especially well dug in and camouflaged, and had come to dominate this portion of the battlefield. By nightfall, the Russian counter-attack, which only consisted of Gerngross' force, had not captured any important objective, partially due to it being a frontal assault, rather than the envelopment it was envisioned to be.

On the night of the 6th, Kuropatkin read what proved to be a false report, stating a Japanese force of 6,000 men was located 15 miles north of Mukden. Kuropatkin's greatest anxiety had long been that his armies' line of retreat would be cut off, and the entire force would be imperilled. Only the emotional protests of Bilderling and Kaulbars were able to talk him down from ordering his southern forces, the 3rd and 1st Manchurian Armies and Rennenkampf, to retreat from the Sha-Ho back to the Hun-Ho on the 6th. For the time being, the Russian lines were left as they were.

In the early hours of 7 March, both Kuropatkin and Kaulbars separately concluded that without further reinforcement, Kaulbars' western-facing force would not be able to successfully counter-attack the Japanese divisions converging on it. Kuropatkin therefore settled on his former course of action to pull his forces on the Sha-Ho back to the line of the Hun-Ho. At 0900hrs, he issued instructions to Linevich and Bilderling to send their heavy artillery back during the day, and as soon as darkness fell that night, to move their troops back through forced marches and with rearguards to the line south of Mukden. Kuropatkin added one further note: 'I may add that I am firmly of opinion that the First Army has done its duty to the last, and that its operations have not been the cause of our retreat to Mukden.'[13] Kuropatkin also ordered Linevich to immediately dispatch the 72nd Division north, from which Kuropatkin hoped to form a new general reserve, to be used in a last attempted counter-attack to decide the battle in the coming days. Meanwhile, Kaulbars ordered his western force and the 2nd Manchurian Army to stand fast. They would soon be severely pressed by the advancing Japanese.

On the 7th, Nogi would nearly envelop Kaulbars' flank. Nogi's 1st Division manoeuvred fully around the Russian right, nearly cutting off the railroad and telegraph lines north of Mukden. Only the redeployment of Birger's mixed infantry and cavalry force in the way of the Japanese advance prevented this. Birger had been positioned further north for the last several days, where his task had been to protect Mukden from that direction. Birger's force did not directly engage the Japanese on the 7th, but positioned itself advantageously to resist the Japanese 1st Division in coming days. Birger's force was integrated with several of Grekov's cavalry regiments, and

Despite setbacks, the Russian soldiers fought steadfastly throughout the war. The Orthodox faith of many doubtless played a role in their stoicism in the face of mortal danger. (Photo by Burton Holmes/Archive Farms/Getty Images)

---

13 British Official History of the Russo-Japanese War, Vol 3, 543.

Kuropatkin began referring to this collected force as the 'Northern Front'. Von der Launitz, having been left without a command since the 5th, was put in charge of this. To the south of the Japanese 1st Division, the Japanese 9th Division also began enveloping the Russians by pushing back De Witt's division towards Mukden. By the end of the day, the 'Northern Front' connected with De Witt's division on the north flank of the Russian line and the rest of Kaulbars' force formed almost a semi-circle as it wrapped around the western and south-western approaches to the city of Mukden.

The other elements of Nogi's army were not as lucky as the 1st and 9th Divisions, as the 7th Division assaulted the 1st Siberian Corps head-on and was repulsed with severe loss. The 1st Siberian Corps resolutely held its ground in another action where it completely destroyed a brigade from Oku's 3rd Division. The Japanese brigade had attacked and gained a span of trenches in the centre of the Russian lines, but was swiftly counter-attacked from all sides. Only 400 men of this brigade returned to the Japanese lines. This was part of a more general engagement whereby the 3rd Japanese Division was assaulting the portion of the Russian line held primarily by Topornin's division, which manned a strong position of villages, redoubts and trenches. Attack and counter-attack transpired here throughout the day. This fighting seems to have been the most bloody of the entire battle. In addition to the severe Japanese losses, the British *Official History* of the war cites 5,500 Russians as killed or wounded west of Mukden on 7 March.

Further south, Oku's other divisions continued to assault the Russian lines, generally pushing the southern portion of 2nd Manchurian Army steadily north. With the exception of the remainder of those of Linevich and Rennenkampf, all the Russian forces were converging on Mukden by the night of 7/8 March.

Holding fast in the centre and east
In the centre of the battlefield, 4 March was marked by noticeably less activity than the previous week. On the Russian side, this seemed partially due to a sense that soon they would be ordered to fall back, with some heavy artillery pieces already being transported to Mukden. On the Japanese side, officers expected that Nogi would soon enter Mukden, thereby bringing an end to the battle.

On 5 March, Nodzu's force suffered some unnecessary casualties when his 4th Division attempted to maintain pressure on the recently withdrawn 5th Siberian Corps and suffered 500 casualties. Meanwhile, his 'Okubo' Kobi Division also tried to advance, acting on faulty intelligence that the Russian 6th Siberian Corps in front of it had withdrawn. The 'Okubo' Kobi Division advanced until the Russians suddenly opened fire across their front, quickly inflicting 1,600 casualties on the Kobi troops and forcing them back.

Further to the Japanese right, Kuroki also attacked strongly fortified positions in an effort to maintain pressure on the Russians. His 10th Division made a dawn attack that lasted all day, in spite of Russian machine-gun fire wreaking havoc on his advancing infantry. At nightfall, this assault was also called off, with the 10th Division having lost 2,600. Further to the east, the Japanese 11th Division renewed its attacks against Rennenkampf, which stretched the Russian defenders thin. At one point in the fighting, a single Russian field artillery battery proved critical in plugging a hole in the line and defeating a Japanese attack – testifying to the strain on Rennenkampf's troops.

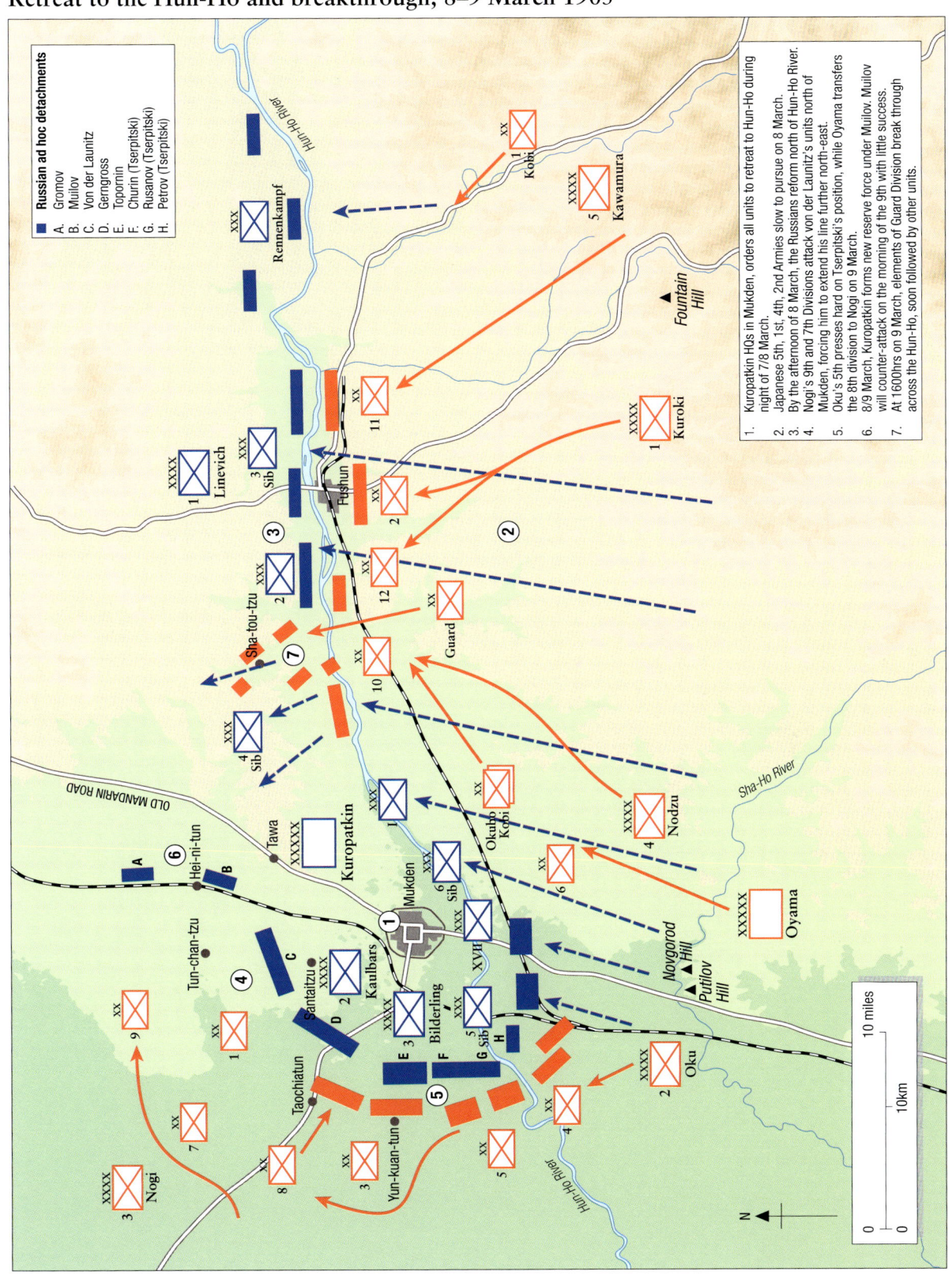

Retreat to the Hun-Ho and breakthrough, 8–9 March 1905

On 6 March, the Japanese 4th Army merely bombarded the centre, especially the area around Putilov Hill. Seemingly, Nodzu had given up on the prospect of seizing these formidable fortifications, merely wishing to wait until Nogi's attack or some other portion of the battle would force Bilderling to withdraw. It should be noted that the Japanese were still employing their heavy siege guns, including 11in howitzers, while the Russian heavy artillery had been somewhat prematurely withdrawn back to Mukden (despite Kuropatkin not yet having ordered a withdrawal). Further east, on Kuroki's right flank, his 2nd Division had extended itself to where it made contact with the Yalu Army. The creation of a contiguous front seemed to have renewed Kawamura's resolve to break Rennenkampf's line, and the Japanese began to bombard and attack at noon on the 6th. Rennenkampf's badly worn regiments continued to hold and at one point captured two machine guns when the Japanese attackers retreated in disorder. Rennenkampf was constantly pulling battalions from less-threatened parts of his line in order to shore up the hardest-pressed positions. By late evening, he telegraphed Danilov – who had not been attacked on the 6th – requesting a battalion be transferred to his position. Somewhat selfishly, Danilov replied that unless the request be made an order, he would not send it, due to anxieties about his own position's strength. Rennenkampf's detachment fended off four more attacks during the night of 6/7 March.

On 7 March, the centre of the front was strangely quiet. Linevich was preparing for the withdrawal to the Hun-Ho that night, having received Kuropatkin's order during the day. The Japanese seemed to expect as much, and contented themselves to let their adversary abandon their formidable positions without further fighting. In the east, this was not the case. The Yalu Army seemed intent to destroy Rennenkampf's detachment, and attacked him throughout the 7th. Rennenkampf resorted to dismounting his Cossack units and inserting them as infantry units in the line as needed. The lines held, and late in the day Russian mounted patrols claimed to have seen Japanese supply columns moving south, implying Kawamura was preparing for a retreat. It is quite possible that these cavalry reports were accurate, but almost simultaneously to hearing these reports, Rennenkampf received Kuropatkin's orders to fall back to the Hun-Ho – rendering the cavalry report a moot point.

PHASE V – DEFENSE OF MUKDEN, 8 MARCH

Retreat to Mukden
Rennenkampf executed an efficient and organized retreat to the Hun-Ho. He started his withdrawal immediately after dusk on 7 March, leaving four battalions, three squadrons and eight machine guns as a rearguard. He continued his retrograde movement in stages, with Danilov's and other smaller elements included in the plan. Rennenkampf's entire force was able to make it to the Hun-Ho by mid-afternoon on 8 March. It covered over 35km in less than 24 hours, which was a remarkable feat in view of the fighting of recent weeks and the need to secure against pursuit. The Japanese Yalu Army did not realize that Rennenkampf's entire force had retreated until 0800hrs, at which point it began a pursuit, though without any significant contact or fighting.

Discounting prisoners, the Japanese numbers of killed and wounded were not much lower than the Russians. Here, Russian soldiers survey the dead of the enemy. (DEA/BIBLIOTECA AMBROSIANA/Contributor)

Linevich and Bilderling's retreats were less orderly. This was partially due to their elements being larger, and in many spots they were retreating from positions that were in very close contact with the enemy. There was much refuse and scattered supplies and equipment left in their wake, and the Japanese pursuit was partially hampered by the long-suffering Japanese infantrymen procuring needed items en route. Nevertheless, the 1st and 3rd Manchurian Armies were also able to execute their retreats in less than 24 hours, without serious interference by the Japanese 1st and 4th Armies. Linevich's army, like that of Rennenkampf, crossed the Hun-Ho and occupied prepared defensive positions facing south across the river. Bilderling's army connected with 2nd Manchurian Army south of the Hun-Ho, where it would protect the southern approaches to the city of Mukden. Kuroki and Nodzu realized the Russians were retreating earlier than Kawamura had, and some of their troops were already occupying the Russian positions by midnight on 7/8 March. However, they did not conduct an aggressive pursuit and did not destroy or even hamper the retreating Russians. Contemporaries and observers were critical of Kuroki and Nodzu for not pressing the pursuit, thereby missing an opportunity to destroy half of Kuropatkin's armies south of the Hun-Ho. However, this should be weighed against not just the exhaustion of the combatants but experiences in recent days of confident Japanese units hastily advancing into still-manned Russian positions. Nodzu's 'Okubo' Kobi Division pursued very slowly, not seriously pressing Bilderling's rearguard throughout its retreat. However, the 'Okubo' Division was at only 60 per cent strength, as it had suffered 4,000 casualties in the last week of fighting. In conducting the pursuit at all, it had to leave 1,000 of its unburied soldiers at the foot of Putilov Hill.

While 1st and 3rd Manchurian Armies were retreating north, Kuropatkin was being severely pressed all around Mukden. Nogi's 3rd Army pressed against von der Launitz's 'Northern Front' and the 2nd Manchurian Army's western-facing units, while Oku attacked the rest of the 2nd Manchurian Army from the south-west and south.

In the north, von der Launitz prepared the 'Northern Front' for defence. He had under his command 26 battalions, 13 squadrons and 72 cannons. During the course of the day, he would continue to be reinforced by more units that Kuropatkin peeled off from the now-arriving 3rd Manchurian Army. Von der Launitz would continuously extend his right flank in a northerly direction, protecting the rail line as the battle front was moving ever closer to it. The attack of the Japanese 1st and 9th Divisions was made somewhat cautiously, with masses of skirmishes advancing while an artillery duel took place. The Japanese were eventually stopped in front of von der Launitz's position, the 9th Division capturing the only village objective of the day and the total force getting no closer than 500 yards from the main Russian positions. Further to the south, Nogi's 7th Division attacked the Russians under Gerngross, but were repulsed without any gain. Oku's 8th and 5th Divisions, which were north of the Hun-Ho and formed a continuous front with Nogi, also attacked the Russian line, but without making any gains. When night fell, the Russian line had held, but Nogi's divisions remained in place all around Mukden, behind what cover the terrain and villages provided and in relatively close proximity to the Russian lines – and the rail line.

Still further to the north-west, Nogi had consolidated his two cavalry brigades into a cavalry division. This formation began to advance upon the underperforming Russian cavalry facing them – the Ural Trans-Baikal Cossack Division under Grekov. Throughout the days, both sides conducted patrols and reconnaissance against each other's positions, though little else transpired. For the Russians, this might be considered a success, as the Japanese cavalry was unable to affect events around Mukden. However, for Kuropatkin, this action represented yet another threat, with the potential to cut the rail line and Kuropatkin's line of communications, supply and retreat.

As night fell on the 8th, Kuropatkin issued his orders. He hedged his bets, telling his armies to prepare for a hasty retreat to Tieh-ling (70km to the north), while he also gave instructions for constituting a new general reserve under Gen Muilov. In terms of preparation for a retreat, he informed his commanders of the precariousness of the situation and the threat to their line of retreat. He therefore ordered them to prepare their troops by packing enough food and water for five or six days, and to plan on taking nothing else but weapons and ammunition in the event a retreat was ordered. In terms of the reserve, Kuropatkin had only five battalions on the night of the 8th, but he issued orders to the armies, especially to Bilderling, for 50 more battalions on the 9th. This force would be commanded by Muilov and was positioned north-east of Mukden, with the intention that it would cooperate with von der Launitz's 'Northern Front'. If Kuropatkin could efficiently assemble and position this force for a counter-attack, he still might be able to parry or even defeat Nogi's Army and thereby neutralize Oyama's main effort.

PHASE V – DEFENSE OF MUKDEN, 9–10 MARCH

Battle for Mukden

In the early morning of 9 March, Muilov wrote back and forth with von der Launitz to coordinate an assault on Nogi's left flank. However, after many hours, von der Launitz replied that he had no forces to spare for such an attack, leaving Muilov to go in alone. Muilov therefore committed to bombard the Japanese positions at 1000hrs and attack at noon. Just as his artillery was initiating its bombardment at 1000hrs, Nogi's 1st Division cautiously began its attack in the same area. After the Russians temporarily checked the Japanese advance with some rifle volleys from the rail line defensive positions, Muilov committed his battalions to attack. Muilov's small force had some success, and in addition to capturing some trenches took two Japanese machine guns. However, a worsening dust storm that day made reinforcement and support of Muilov's force difficult. Meanwhile, further to the north, the Japanese 9th Division successfully attacked and seized two villages, forcing Kuropatkin to call off the attack and focus his forces on defending the rail line.

Further south, Oku's force continued to press the Russian defences with either local attacks or artillery bombardment. To the east, Bilderling and Linevich's armies were content to follow their orders for the day and merely defend in place, overlooking the Hun-Ho. However, there were gaps in their defences, and some of Bilderling's troops noticed columns of the Japanese 6th Division and 'Okubo' Kobi Division moving further east. The gaps in the Russian line were made worse as the day progressed, as battalions were being transferred to Mukden to reconstitute Kuropatkin's reserve. The Japanese front in this sector of the battlefield was also porous, but the Russians did not seem inclined to exploit any gaps, whereas the Japanese divisions were on the move. Beginning around 1600hrs, elements of the Japanese Guards Division, as well as two other divisions, crossed the partially frozen river at several points. Visibility was still low due to the continuing dust storm, and in the sector where the Guards Division crossed, there were only a few companies of Russians covering a front of several kilometres. The Japanese were quick to cross more units after they had a foothold, and in the space of a few hours the entire Guards Division was across. At 1900hrs, small elements of the 'Okubo' Division crossed the river at another point, and were only driven back after a hand grenade battle with elements of 4th Siberian Corps.

Unaware of this dangerous development, Kuropatkin had nevertheless decided that the battle was lost and issued orders to retreat. By 2015hrs, orders were going out to the armies, with Muilov tasked as the rearguard for the army. The plan was tweaked again before 10 March, when Kuropatkin decided that an attack by Muilov's force would have the added benefit of distracting the Japanese forces, allowing 2nd Manchurian Army to extricate itself out of the south and escape. Kuropatkin met with Muilov to discuss this plan at around 2200hrs, then around 2300hrs he received word of the penetration of the Hun-Ho line. At midnight, Kuropatkin modified Muilov's orders, calling off the attack and instead ordering him to conduct the original course of action, to act as the rearguard for the whole army.

During the night of 9/10 March, the situation in Mukden – and especially the railhead – became especially chaotic. The Russians made a concerted effort to evacuate all of their wounded, via train, north to Tieh-ling. Thousands of wounded soldiers were being loaded onto trains of about 50 cars and sent north. Even the generals' railcars were pressed into service to either transport wounded men or the immense quantities of supplies that seemed to lay about everywhere. It should be recalled that the Russian armies had been occupying the positions of the Sha-Ho for some six months, and therefore the build-up of war materiel had been immense. Many fires were started to

THE BATTLE FOR MUKDEN: 9–10 MARCH 1905

After a last attempted Russian counter-attack on 9 March, Kuropatkin orders the retreat of Russian forces north to Tieh-ling. Kuropatkin attempts an extremely difficult military feat – to extricate an army out of corridor between converging enemy pincers. Oyama's armies attempt to complete their victory by destroying the Manchurian 2nd and 3rd Armies in and around the city of Mukden. The result is chaotic, but Kuropatkin escapes with his command intact, though badly disorganized.

RUSSIAN
1. Gromov
2. Lisovski (Muilov)
3. Gershelmann (Muilov)
4. Nekrasov (Von Der Launitz)
5. Sollogub (Von Der Launitz)
6. De Vitt (Von Der Launitz)
7. Lesh (Gerngross)
8. 1 ESRR (Gerngross)
9. 9 ESRR (Kraus/Gerngross)
10. Topornin
11. Churin (Tserpitski)
12. Ganenfeldt (Tserpitski)
13. Rusanov (Tserpitski)
14. 5th Siberian Corps
15. XVII Corps Cavalry Brigade

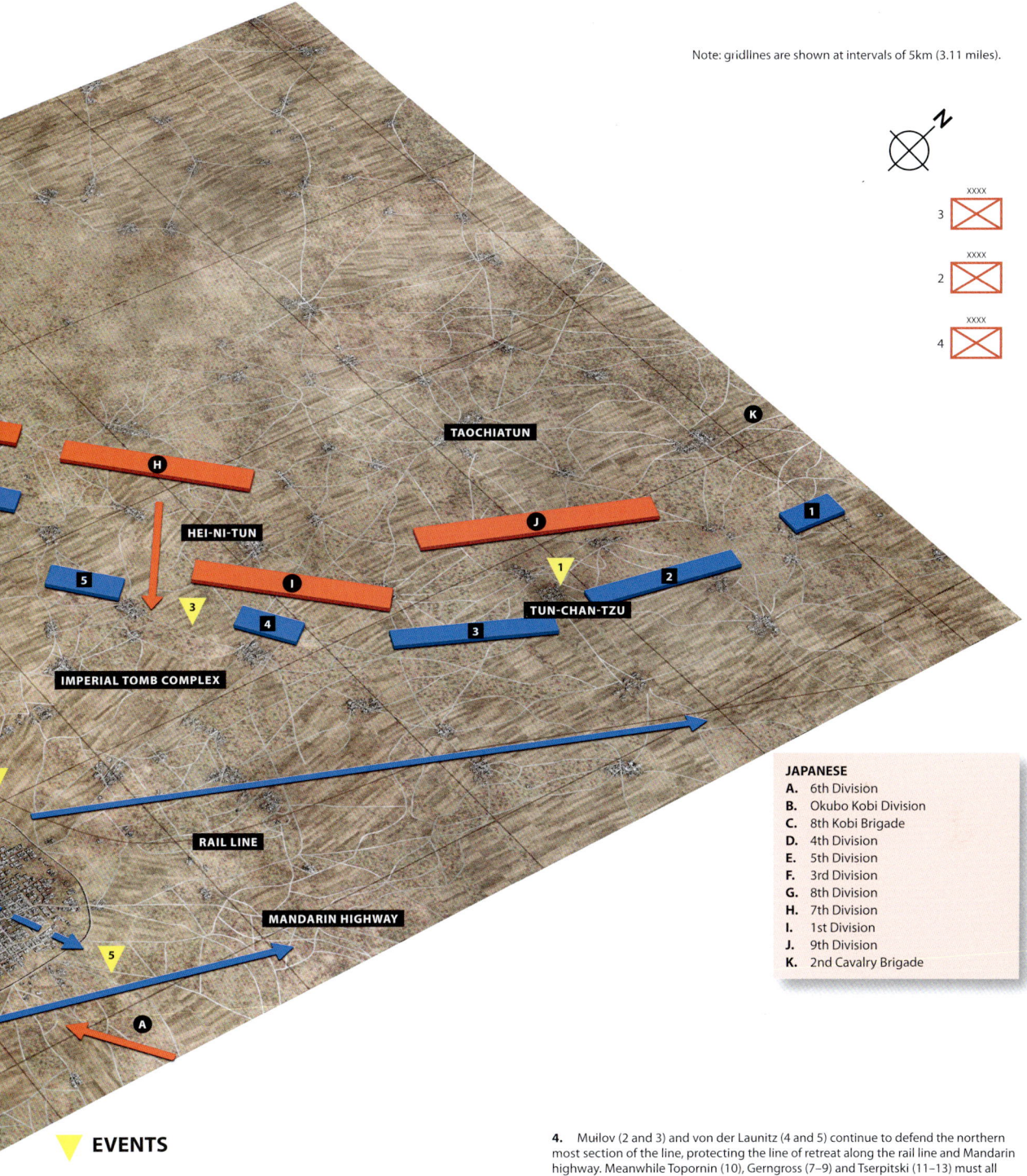

Note: gridlines are shown at intervals of 5km (3.11 miles).

JAPANESE
- A. 6th Division
- B. Okubo Kobi Division
- C. 8th Kobi Brigade
- D. 4th Division
- E. 5th Division
- F. 3rd Division
- G. 8th Division
- H. 7th Division
- I. 1st Division
- J. 9th Division
- K. 2nd Cavalry Brigade

▼ EVENTS

9 March

1. Between 1000hrs and 1200hrs: Muilov (3) attacks with little support and engages the the Japanese 1st Division (I), while the Japanese 9th Division (J) attacks and seizes two villages to the North, endangering Kuropatkin's lines of supply and retreat.

2. Between 1000hrs and 1200hrs: Muilov (3) attacks with little support and engages the Japanese 1st Division (I), while the Japanese 9th Division (J) attacks and seizes two villages to the North, endangering Kuropatkin's lines of supply and retreat.

10 March

3. Before dawn: five battalions of 7th Division breaks Russian line and occupy Tomb Complex. While the Russians counter-attack and reform their battle line, the Japanese in the Tomb Complex barricade themselves in, and will remain there for the rest of the battle.

4. Muilov (2 and 3) and von der Launitz (4 and 5) continue to defend the northern most section of the line, protecting the line of retreat along the rail line and Mandarin highway. Meanwhile Topornin (10), Gerngross (7–9) and Tserpitski (11–13) must all retreat along a narrowing gap IVO Mukden, in order to escape north behind the screen provided by Muilov and von der Launitz. The scene around Mukden is chaotic as divisions of retreating Russian soldiers converge on a few roads.

5. Ganenfeldt (12) provides the rearguard for the rest of Tserpitski's force (11, 13). Ganenfeldt evades Oku's divisions (E, F) by retreating through the city of Mukden itself. While passing through the city, thousands of Russian stragglers join his column, believing it will provide their best chance to escape. Northeast of the city, the Japanese 6th Division (A) is positioned to block Ganenfeldt's retreat. Once it exits the city, Ganenfeldt's force is surrounded and nearly annihilated. The fighting in this stage of the battle is exceptionally bloody as the Russian force is desperate to escape the city of Mukden, but met with enemy rifle and machine gun fire. This engagement accounts for a large portion of the Russian prisoners taken by the Japanese during the Battle of Mukden.

Russian infantry in retreat. This scene would have been commonplace in the two weeks after the battle during the retreats to Tieh-ling and Hsi-ping-kai. (Photo by Ipsumpix/Corbis via Getty Images)

destroy what could not be transported, and any railcar that could not be sent north was also destroyed. Smaller vehicles and civilians clogged the roads heading north. As dawn broke, Kuropatkin would attempt to extricate his nearly 270,000 soldiers from amidst this chaos.

Adding to the chaos was the attack by the Japanese 7th Division on von der Launitz's men north-west of Mukden. It was still dark when five Japanese battalions broke through a portion of the Russian line with the Imperial temple complex located behind it. The Japanese quickly occupied the temple, and while the Russians plugged the hole in their line, they now had a sizeable Japanese force that needed to be eliminated in their rear area. Meanwhile, the fighting expanded to all of Muilov's front and that of von der Launitz. As long as these elements could hold, they would provide the screen that Kuropatkin required, behind which the 2nd Manchurian Army was expected to withdraw in haste. By 1000hrs, all the units of 2nd Manchurian Army were moving, with their own rearguards in place but still heavily reliant on von der Launitz's and Muilov's screen. The retreating Russian brigades selected multiple routes, along which they dispatched their units in numerous columns, with instructions to reconsolidate at various points around Mukden. By this point in the morning, the roads leading north out of Mukden were becoming overwhelmed with traffic; Kuropatkin's force sorely needed additional time to prevent its retreat from becoming a rout. Several Japanese units, such as the 5th Division, did not make any initial attempt to pursue, perhaps simply due to exhaustion after weeks of combat. Later in the day, around 1130hrs, Oku would prompt their pursuit with direct orders. Other units, such as the 6th Division and 'Okubo' Kobi Division, enthusiastically pursued the foe, seeing this as a decisive moment in the battle. Gen Okubo personally led his soldiers forward.

This was all happening west of the Japanese penetration of the Hun-Ho line. East of this, Linevich and Rennenkampf began their retreat, essentially due north. Their routes would not be the Mandarin highway that the rest of the Russians were using, but they would plan to converge at Tieh-ling once they had escaped the Japanese columns. The Japanese Guards Division had set itself on a north-westward advance, with the intention of cutting off Kuropatkin's retreat through linking up with Nogi's 3rd Army north of Mukden. By about noon on 10 March, Nogi's army and elements of Kuroki's army were separated by some 12km, in both cases with Russians contesting their advance. For the time being, Kuropatkin therefore had a 12km-wide gap through which to pull out his army.

The order by which Russian units retreated out of the Mukden envelopment is difficult to relay, as the Russian units had by this stage in the battle been severely intermingled by Kuropatkin's constant unit-organizational changes. Various division size-elements were fighting under Muilov, von der Launitz, Topornin, Tserpitski, Lesh and others. Out of all of 2nd and 3rd Armies, only the 1st Siberian Corps and XVII Corps were still operating as mostly organic corps. The rest of the Russian units were operating as amalgamated brigades, and even these were beginning to break down. Generally, the forces to move first were those south of Mukden, then south-east, followed by those south-west and lastly south-west of Mukden.

This breakdown in order was especially true south of Mukden, where columns of retreating soldiers were beginning to intermingle. Too many units attempted to use too few routes, resulting in scenes of chaos. At one such choke point, a few kilometres north of Mukden, observers noted thousands of Russian soldiers intermixed with vehicles on the road, seemingly without any officers directing them. Scattered shrapnel shots added urgency, but not efficiency, to the crowds of men, animals and vehicles. In cases such as these, unit integrity broke down completely, crowds of men simply attempting to move north towards presumed safety.

To the east, Rennenkampf and Linevich were able to retreat without serious issue. Their own internal rearguards kept the Japanese at bay and enabled their forces to make their way north without threat to their survival. Rennenkampf did not actually begin his retreat until 1600hrs, before which his rearguard was able to repel one more Japanese 11th Division probe. To the west, the Russian situation was more desperate. Surprisingly, the majority of the 2nd and 3rd Manchurian Armies were able to escape Oyama's envelopment by around 1600hrs, though in great disorder.

Between 1600hrs and 1900hrs, the remaining Russian rearguards and screens began to cave in around Mukden. Von der Launitz and Muilov were gradually enveloped from the south, their left flank, and pushed north beginning about noon. At 1600hrs, the rest of the Japanese 7th Division broke through the Russian lines and secured the Chinese temple, liberating its battalions that had been besieged inside the complex since earlier that morning. To the north, 1st Division pushed against the Russian lines until it seized the railroad position at around 1800hrs. Around this time, there was one instance of

This photograph of Kuropatkin's retreat captures the chaos of mixed formations, combat troops, supply and civilian transport all intermingled. (From a Photographic Record of the Russo-Japanese War, P. F. Collier & Son, 1905, via Wikimedia Commons)

Overview of the Manchurian theatre, April–September 1905

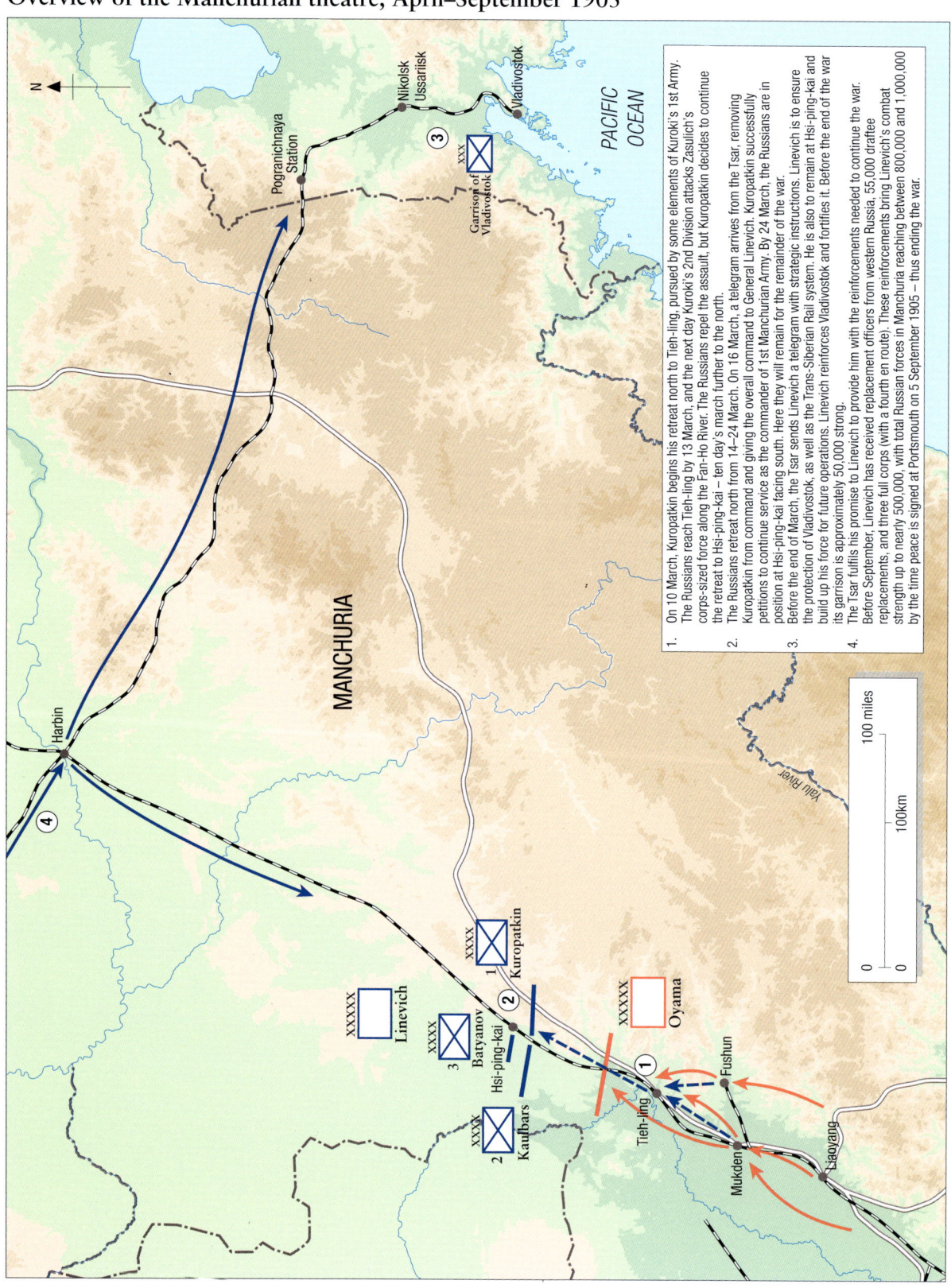

mass surrender, when a column of perhaps 15,000 Russians emerged, by some accounts including many intoxicated soldiers and civilians, out of the northern exits of the city. The more organized elements of this force were the remaining units of Tserpitski's assigned rearguard force under Gen Ganenfeldt, which had made its way into the city of Mukden to avoid converging Japanese troops south of the city. While this force was making its way through the city, it drew into its ranks many stragglers and individual soldiers who were left behind or separated from their units. They must have believed that the discipline and order of Ganenfeld's force represented potential salvation from the developing Japanese 'pocket' closing in around them. Unfortunately for these men, the Japanese 6th Division, manning positions north-east of the city, had already cut off Ganenfeldt's 'route' out of Mukden. A brigade of the Japanese 6th Division, originally moving north, turned south and arrayed itself defensively to block the Russians' movement north. A furious engagement followed, in which the Japanese engaged the Russian column with rifle fire and machine guns. Those Russian units still organized enough to manoeuvre attempted to break out. Immense carnage ensued, during which perhaps 5,000 Russians were killed and wounded. Some of the Russians immediately surrendered, while the remainder of the force scattered, moving in battalion and brigade sized elements, still attempting to escape the pocket. It took many hours, lasting into 11 March, for the 6th Division to collect the majority of these as prisoners – as many as 10,000 in all. Between the 10th and 11th, a further group of 2,500 Russians was captured further to the north-east, consisting of Bilderling's troops who were resisting the westward movement of the Japanese Guards Division.

PHASE VI – RETREAT, 11–20 MARCH

The Russian retreat
Despite the fates of units like that of Ganenfeldt, Kuropatkin's plan of retreat had essentially worked. By 9 and 10 March, the Russian position around Mukden had become untenable. Despite converging Japanese armies from the west and south, nearly surrounding the 2nd and 3rd Manchurian Armies in the city of Mukden, and Nogi's army assaulting Kuropatkin's line of retreat along the rail line, the various Russian detachments had held. Though Oyama and his staff had planned and executed the battle brilliantly, Oyama had only defeated Kuropatkin in yet another field engagement, falling short of the total victory he had sought. The only units to be trapped in Oyama's 'cauldron' and destroyed were elements of the various Russian rearguards. The vast majority of the soldiers of the Russian Manchurian armies, though disorganized and badly demoralized, were quickly moving north to Tieh-ling, where they would consolidate in new defensive positions.

Rennenkampf and Linevich continued a controlled retreat in the east, converging towards Tieh-ling, while the 2nd and 3rd Manchurian Armies with Kuropatkin remained disordered, lumbering north throughout 11 March. For the entire day, hundreds of thousands of Russians and accompanying non-combatants, animals and baggage carts merely clambered northward towards Tieh-ling. There, security was provided by three organized rearguard units, two of which guarded against Japanese pursuit up the railway line and a third protected the Russian rear along the Mandarin highway. The Japanese cavalry was unable to exploit the retreat, as the Russian cavalry was still relatively fresh and numerically superior. The most effective pursuit was conducted by the infantry divisions of Kuroki's 1st Army. Oku's and Nodzu's armies, meanwhile, consolidated around Mukden, while Nogi's forces reorganized still further north of the city. Kawamura's force occupied the former positions of Rennenkampf, but did not press the pursuit. On 12 March, there was very little contact and the Russians were able to begin occupying Tieh-ling.

By 13 March, a corps-sized force from the 2nd Manchurian Army was in position along the Fan-Ho River, just south of Tieh-ling, providing security for the retreating armies who continued to pass through on their way to Tieh-ling. Kuropatkin appointed Gen Zasulich to command the defences along the Fan-Ho. Zasulich had been the Russian battlefield commander at the first battle of the war along the Yalu River.

Kuropatkin ordered the armies to prepare to defend in the Fan-Ho position and give battle south of Tieh-ling. Kuroki's 2nd and 12th Divisions had advanced to positions just south of the Fan-Ho River, where they made contact with a regiment of the Russian rearguard on the 13th. On 14 March, the 2nd Division attacked Zasulich in strength. After a morning artillery bombardment, the Japanese attacked over the frozen river and attempted to scale the heights on which the Russian defenders were emplaced. The Russians seemed to have made especially effective use of grenades in this fighting, and despite gaining at least one regiment-sized foothold, the Japanese called off the attack after a few hours. Later that day, Kuropatkin met with his staff to evaluate his armies' dispositions. The reports of his staff painted a bleak picture of insufficient ammunition, food and other supplies. After making a new assessment of his forces' ability to fight at the Tiehling position, Kuropatkin changed his mind and renewed the retreat.

On 14 March, Kuropatkin ordered his armies north to the rail station at Hsi-ping-kai, a ten-day march of roughly 100 miles. The armies would continue their retreat, bounding by army to defensive positions along the way, thereby securing the march of the rearguard. On 16 March, a telegram arrived at Kuropatkin's headquarters detailing his removal from command and the appointment of Linevich as commander of the armies in Manchuria. Two days later, Kuropatkin successfully petitioned the tsar and was able to assume a role as a subordinate commander, in Linevich's former billet as commander of the 1st Manchurian Army. During the ten-day retreat from Tieh-ling, there was no further close pursuit by, or fights with, Kuroki's 12th and 2nd Divisions. By 24 March, the Russians arrived in Hsi-ping-kai, where they renewed their efforts to reorganize and re-equip.

Linevich's first act as commander of the armies was to order them into new positions defending Hsi-ping-kai. The 1st Manchurian Army, now under Kuropatkin, still with Rennenkampf's detachment on its flank, would occupy the left flank, facing south-east of the rail line. The 2nd Manchurian Army, with Mishchenko's cavalry, would form the right flank, west of the rail line. The 3rd Manchurian Army would serve as Linevich's reserve. The Russians would remain in this position and general disposition for the remainder of the war.

AFTERMATH

MASSING IN MANCHURIA

In late March, Tsar Nicholas II telegrammed Linevich with instructions for how the war should be carried out in the coming months. In short, Linevich was to ensure lines of communication with Vladivostok, Harbin and Europe were maintained and protected, the Trans-Siberian Railway would continue to be guarded and maintained, and Linevich would receive reinforcement at his current position.

Linevich assessed that he would need at least 150,000 additional troops to be ready for renewed combat. Currently he had only 225,000 or so combat troops, though the total Russian troop strength may have been twice that if support and rear-echelon troops are included. Linevich voiced a strong preference to prioritize reinforcement by units, rather than individual draftee replacements. This would be difficult, as replacement by unit was more complicated for the Russian War Ministry, units requiring three times as much time in Russia to consolidate and train as individual replacements. Next, Linevich needed to replace his lost officers. Whereas the cavalry regiments were only 1 per cent short of their authorized officer strength, infantry units were short of their authorized strength by 43 per cent. To address this shortage, the War Ministry placed 2,200 Russian infantry officers in western Russia on orders to join Linevich in Manchuria.

The first wave of 55,000 soldiers to arrive at Hsi-ping-kai consisted almost entirely of individual replacements. However, the tsar eventually wholeheartedly fulfilled Linevich's earlier request for units. In the coming months, on top of individual replacements, Linevich would receive three further European corps (the IV, IX and XIX), while a fourth, the XIII Corps, was on its way when peace was concluded in September 1905. These new formations were noticeably better uniformed and equipped, and generally consisted of better-quality soldiers and officers than had been the norm in Manchuria up to this point. By late summer, Linevich's strength swelled to 446,000 infantry and 27,000 cavalry, to which many more support troops can be added. In all, the Russians had nearly 800,000 troops under Linevich at the war's end. These numbers were achievable due to additional reservist mobilization waves, which the tsar initiated well after the battle of Mukden. The final mobilization waves of the war, the eighth and ninth, occurred in July 1905 and were some of the most substantial – summoning nearly 300,000 additional men. Either for the purpose of returning to active campaigning or for posturing while peace negotiations unfolded, the tsar decided to fully resource the effort in the Far East until the end of the war.

These mobilizations, concentrations and preparations demonstrate both the weakness and strength of the late Russian Empire. The ground war between March 1904 and March 1905 had been the centre of global military attention for a year, and had witnessed the implementation of cutting-edge technology, tactics and operational manoeuvre. With the battle of Mukden, it also witnessed the greatest land battle in history to that point. Nonetheless, much of the Russian failure was a logistical one as well as a failure of prioritization. Due to competing security requirements and threats to its enormous land border in Europe, the Caucasus and Central Asia, as well as concerns about internal security and order, the tsar was slow to recognize the magnitude of the threat posed by Japan and the quantity of military resources that would be required to meet it. By September 1905, although Russia was on a war footing, less than 50 per cent of its active and activated reservists were with Linevich in Manchuria. Japan had chosen well its time to strike, as the entirety of the Trans-Siberian Railway was continuously improved throughout the war. Despite the difficulties of war conditions, traffic capacity of the railway increased from nine two-way trains a day to 14 by the conflict's end. Had the Japanese delayed and allowed the Russians to continue developing their Eastern railways in peace, the capacity may well have enabled a much more rapid transference of army corps to Manchuria.

The Japanese also continued to reinforce their troops in Manchuria. Before the end of the war, three more regular divisions would be formed and sent to the front (the 14th, 15th and 16th Divisions). However, the quality of Japanese recruits had noticeably declined. The massive losses among the officer corps were the most difficult to replace. Nonetheless, Japanese strength increased in Manchuria, perhaps reaching 370,000 troops in position south of Hsi-ping-kai by the autumn of 1905.

CONCLUSION

In his notes on his combat experience in Manchuria, Russian officer Captain Soloviev noted that a 'characteristic of modern combat' was 'the tenacity and duration of infantry combats without decisive results'.[14] In short, ferocious miniature battles such as at San-de-pu, Redoubt 16 or any of the countless fights between Rennenkampf and the Japanese 11th Division could be won or lost without decisively altering the course of the overall battle. The space and numbers on the battlefield seemed to have outgrown the ability of a spirited charge, or of a cunning brigade or division commander to break through or flank an army, rendering its position untenable or breaking its morale. Even in the event of overwhelming local success, an army's flank might consist of a dozen kilometres of hills or trenches, rendering exploitation a days-long process, especially since the enemy would actively shift reserves to impede such progress. Moreover, battlefields had become 'empty'; that is, when not actively assaulting, there would likely be no visible enemy formations. To reveal your unit's position was to invite rapid, effective artillery fire, even at ranges up to 6km. Therefore, the position of the attacker, especially the

---

14 L. Z. Soloviev, *Actual Experiences in War; Impressions of a Company Commander* (Washington: War Department, 1906), 21–22.

locally successful attacker, would be revealed to all parties, potentially resulting in the reallocation of artillery from multiple formations within 6km to concentrate fire on the, up to this point, successful attacking units.

Marshal Oyama seemed to find the solution at the operational level of war – an attacking army must attack at all points along the front, and aggressively so, in order to preoccupy front-line units, artillery and especially reserves across the whole front. Under these conditions, a defending army cannot risk transferring units every time a local breakthrough occurs, at least without causing chaos to its task organization and rear areas. While successful at Mukden, Oyama's aggressive approach also guaranteed enormous casualties for even a victorious army. All units had to be engaged in the attack, to cause the defender to question whether every sector was the location of the attacker's main effort. This was the case at Mukden, where Oyama's force suffered 70,000 casualties, nearly all killed and wounded. Kuropatkin's force suffered nearly the same number of killed and wounded, but as the defeated army, suffered an additional 20,000–25,000 captured, mostly in the last 24–48 hours of combat.

Despite the unmitigated naval disaster at Tsushima at the end of May, peace was not signed until September. While the lack of a navy after May 1905 and the growing revolutionary movement across Russia since February advocated against continuing the war, the presence of a massive army group in Manchuria was a credible threat to the Japanese position. Linevich's armies were useful in the event of continuing the war, but even more useful as a bargaining chip while diplomats resolved the war. Since August 1905, Minister Sergei Witte had been negotiating an end to the war at Portsmouth, New Hampshire, as US President Theodore Roosevelt had offered himself as mediator for Russia and Japan. The Japanese government, for its part, was looking for a quick end to the war. The financial cost of 18 months of large-scale industrial conflict on land and sea had been nearly ruinous, and without loans from its ally (since 1902) Great Britain, the war would have ended much sooner and potentially less favourably for Japan. In this context, Japanese diplomats signed a relatively lenient peace with the Russian Empire – notably not requiring the payment of an indemnity. There was considerable public outcry at home, given the massive sacrifice borne by the Japanese people to achieve the victory. However, the Japanese officials were pragmatic, electing to affirm their moderate gains rather than risk them in continued conflict.

Casualties of the armies at Mukden

Army	Killed	Wounded	MIA	Total
Japanese 1st Army (Kuroki)	1925	8818	N/A	**10473**
Japanese 2nd Army (Oku)	5093	13084	N/A	**18177**
Japanese 3rd Army (Nogi)	4585	13938	N/A	**18523**
Japanese 4th Army (Nodzu)	3691	13197	N/A	**16888**
Japanese 5th Army (Kawamura)	1529	4439	N/A	**5698**
Total	**16553**	**53476**	**N/A**	**70029**
1st Manchurian Army (Linevich)	3483	17687	3515	**24685**
2nd Manchurian Army (Kaulbars)	3369	21013	16799	**41181**
3rd Manchurian Army (Bilderling)	1853	12688	9016	**23557**
Total	**8705**	**51388**	**29330**	**89423**

Data derived from Sergey N. Biryuk, *Russkaya pekhota v Russko-yaponskoy voyne 1904–1905* (*Russian Infantry in the Russo-Japanese War 1904–1905*) (Moscow: Eksmo, 2021), 350, 352.

THE BATTLEFIELD TODAY

Mukden was the ancient capital of Manchuria and the name itself is Manchu. Today it is called Shenyang, and it is still one of the largest and most important cities in north-eastern China. In 1905, American observers and others noted the dense population of the region around Mukden, with walled villages scattered throughout the countryside and cultivated land covering the only space in between. Over the course of the 20th century, however, industry boomed, changing the nature of the city and the region. The old city, a walled settlement about 5km across, has expanded into a sprawling metropolis of 9 million people, with 23 million living in the greater metropolitan area. This growth has covered much of the area fought over in 1905, especially the combat around the city of Mukden itself. South of the city, particularly along the Sha-Ho River, the area is less developed and

Shenyang (Mukden) has grown into a sprawling city of millions, covering much of the old battlefield. The eastern flank of the battlefield and parts of the Sha-Ho front are still relatively undisturbed.

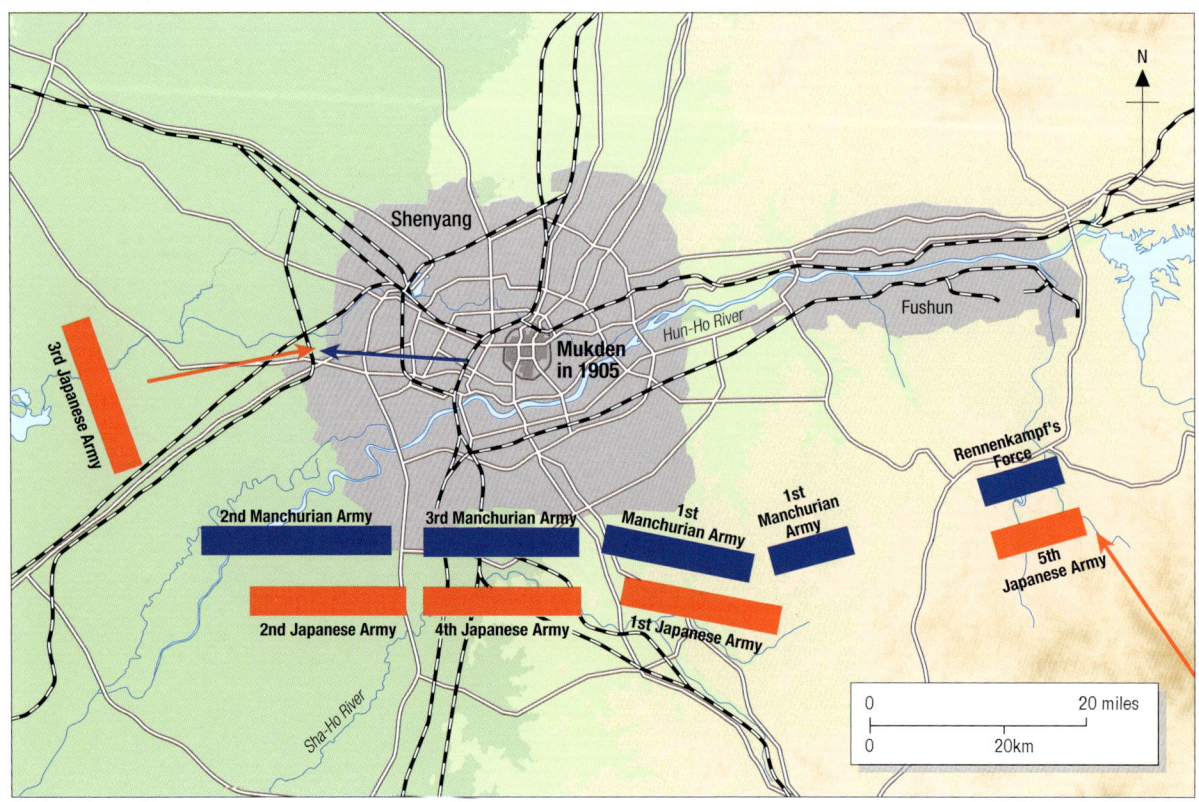

an appreciation of the terrain and the fighting that transpired there is still possible. The spur of Redoubt 16 still bears the scars of trenches and the Russian fortifications. Hei-kou-tai and San-de-pu retain their 1905 names, and though larger than they were 100 years ago, are still surrounded by agricultural land, similar to that over which Russian and Japanese battalions attacked and counter-attacked in January 1905.

The geopolitical nature of the Russo-Japanese War and the battle of Mukden have impaired their remembrance. The battle was fought between Russia and Japan, but located in China. Moreover, the war took place during a period China remembers as a 'century of humiliation'. Russia lost the battle and has not sought to extensively memorialize it, whereas Japan may not do so due to the memory of a later Mukden Incident in 1933 and war in Manchuria superseding the earlier 1905 battle in historical memory. For political and historical reasons, it is not possible for Japan to memorialize a glorious victory through which it came to dominate the region.

However, there are some enduring attractions connected to the battle. The current Shenyang Railway Station was built in 1899 by the Russians of the Chinese Eastern Railway, and the eastern entrance is the original architecture, clearly in the Russian style. This was the site of much traffic throughout the war, particularly during the February and March battle. Perhaps of greater note is the Zhaoling complex of the Qing Dynasty. A site of cultural and historical importance even at the time of the battle, it was also the site of active fighting during the battle when, on 10 March, Japanese regiments of Nogi's army broke through the Russian lines in the area and successfully barricaded themselves into the complex. The tomb complex and surrounding areas are now a UNESCO World Heritage Site and are well maintained for tourism.

Photographed in 1905, these were the tombs where several Japanese battalions barricaded themselves in on the last day of battle, 10 March 1905. (Author's collection)

FURTHER READING

Primary Source Records

Kuropatkin, Aleksey Nikolayevich, *The Russian Army and the Japanese War: Being Historical and Critical Comments on the Military Policy and Power of Russia and on the Campaign in the Far East* (trans Capt A. B. Lindsay), John Murray, London (1909)

Palmer, Frederick, *With Kuroki in Manchuria*, Charles Scribner's Sons, New York (1904)

Reports of Military Officers Attached to the Armies in Manchuria during the Russo-Japanese War, United States War Department General Staff (1906–07)

Soloviev, L. Z., 34th East Siberian Regiment, *Actual Experiences in War: Battle Action of the Infantry: Impressions of a Company Commander*, Government Printing Office, Washington, DC (1906)

Official Sources

The Official History of the Russo-Japanese War, Part III: The Battle of Mukden, Historical Section of the Committee of Imperial Defense, HMSO, London (1909)

The Russo-Japanese War, Part I: From Yinkou to Sandepu, and *Part V: The Battle of Mukden*, Historical Section of the German General Staff (trans Karl von Donat), Hugh Rees Ltd, London (1914)

Secondary Sources

Biryuk, Sergey N, *Russkaya pekhota v Russko-yaponskoy voyne 1904–1905* (Russian Infantry in the Russo-Japanese War 1904–1905), Eksmo, Moscow (2021)

Connaughton, Richard, *Rising Sun and Tumbling Bear: Russia's War with Japan*, Cassell, London (2003)

Corbett, Sir Julien S., *Maritime Operations in the Russo Japanese War*, volumes I–II, Naval Institute Press, Annapolis (1994) (first published in 1914)

Donat, Karl von, *The Russo Japanese War 1904–1905: The Battle of Mukden*, Hugh Rees, London (1908)

Forczyk, Robert, *Port Arthur 1904–1905: The First Modern Siege*, Osprey Publishing, Oxford (2024)

Fuller, William C., *Strategy and Power in Russia, 1600–1914*, Free Press, New York (1992)

Ivanov, A. and Jowett, P., *The Russo-Japanese War 1904–1905*, Osprey Publishing, Oxford (2004)

Menning, Bruce W., *Bayonets Before Bullets: The Imperial Russian Army, 1861–1914*, University of Indiana Press, Indianapolis (1992)

Paine, S. C. M., *The Japanese Empire: Grand Strategy from the Meiji Restoration to the Pacific War*, Cambridge University Press, Cambridge (2017)

Paine, S. C. M., *The Sino-Japanese War of 1894–1895: Perceptions, Power, and Primacy*, Cambridge University Press, Cambridge (2005)

Reese, Roger R., *The Imperial Russian Army in Peace, War, and Revolution 1856–1917*, University Press of Kansas, Lawrence (2017)

Tadayoshi, Sakurai, *Human Bullets: A Soldier's Story of the Russo-Japanese War*, University of Nebraska Press, Lincoln (1999)

Steinberg, John W., 'Imperial War Games (1898–1906): Symbolic Displays of Power or Practical Training?' in *The Military and Society in Russia 1450–1917* (ed Eric Lohr and Marshall Poe), Brill, Leiden (2002)

Walder, David, *The Short Victorious War: The Russo-Japanese Conflict 1904–1905*, Harper and Row, New York (1974)

Warner, Denis and Warner, Peggy, *The Tide at Sunrise: A History of the Russo-Japanese War 1904–1905*, Charterhouse, New York (1974)

INDEX

aftermath 89–90
Aleksandrovich, Grand Duke Sergei 5
Alexeiv, Lt Gen 43, 44, 46, 47, 49

Baumgarten, Maj Gen 31, 52
Beresnev Hill 44, 46
Bezobrazov, Aleksandr 7
Bilderling, Aleksandr Aleksandrovich 19, 24, 66, 71, 72, 75, 79, 80, 81, 87
Boxer Rebellion 7, 22, 23, 24

campaign
 assault on Fountain Hill 53, **53**
 battle for Fountain Hill 67, **68–70**, 71
 Battle for Mukden 80–81, **82–83**, 84–85, **84**, **85**, 87, 90
 Beresnev Hill 44, 46
 casualties and losses 44, 47, 57, 63, 64, 65, 71, 72, 76, 79, **79**, 87, 90, 91
 Deniken Hill 44, 46
 diversionary attack 41, 43–45, **46**, 47, 49
 initial positions 42
 Japanese artillery bombardment, 28 February **54–56**, 57–58, **57**
 Nogi's envelopment 58, **58**, 63, 63–66
 phase I, 19–26 February 43–45, **46**, 47, 49
 phase II, 27–28 February **48**, 49, **50–51**, 52–53, **53**, **54–56**, 57–58, **57**, **58**, 59, **60–62**, 63
 phase III, 1–3 March 63–67, **68–70**, 71
 phase IV, 4–7 March 71–76, **72**, 78
 phase V, 77, 9–10 March 80–81, **82–83**, 84–85, **84**, **85**, 87
 phase VI, 11–20 March 87–88
 Putilov Hill 57, 67, 78
 redoubts captured 67
 Rennenkampf Hill 46
 retreat to Mukden 78–80
 retreat to the Hun-Ho 75, **77**, 78, 78–79
 Russian counter-attack 64–66
 Russian counter-attack on the Western Flank 71–76, **72**
 Russian defensive line 42
 Russian retreat 4, 84–85, **84**, **85**, 87, 87–88
 storming of Redoubt 16: **50–51**, 52
 terrain 42, **42**, 53, 65
 weather 44, 64
casualties and losses 10, 14, 19, 30, 44, 47, 57, 63, 64, 71, 72, 76, 79, **79**, 87, 90, 91

Chemulpo 10, 11
Chenghocheng 41, 43
China 6–7, 93
China Eastern Railway 7
chronology 20–21

Dalny 10
Danilov, Maj Gen 49, 52, 67, 71, 78
Deniken Hill 44, 46
diversionary attack 41, 43–45, **46**, 47, 49

Evert, Maj Gen Aleksei 13

Fan-Ho River 88
firepower 29
Fountain Hill, assault on 53, **53**
Fountain Hill, battle for 67, **68–70**, 71
Franco-Prussian War 25

Gerngross, Lt Gen 35, 73–75, 80
Grand Manoeuvres, Kursk, 1902 4, 5, 8
Grekov, Maj Gen 58, **60–62**, 63
Grippenberg, Gen 15, 18–19, 24

Hei-Kou-Tai 15, 18, 93
horses 73
Hsi-ping-kai 88, 89
Hun-Ho River 42, 43, 52, 81
 retreat to 75, **77**, 78, 78–79

Imperial Japanese Army
 artillery 8, **15**, 33, **46**, **54–56**, 57–58, **57**
 cavalry 31, 33, **33**
 commanders 24–26, **25**, **26**
 logistics 12
 order of battle 36–37
 organization 32, 33
 replacements 33
 strength 7, 31, 37, 90
 uniforms **12**, 29
 weapons 32–33, **32**
Imperial Japanese Army formation
 1st Army 10, 25, 26, 36, 40, 41, 47, 49, 79, 88
 1st Cavalry Brigade 63
 1st Division 58, **60–62**, 63, 73, 75–76, 80, 81, 85
 1st Kobi Division 15, 41, 44, 49, 53
 2nd Army 10–11, 18–19, **18**, 26, 36–37, 41, 47, 63, 64, 65–66, 72
 2nd Cavalry Brigade 58, 63, 66
 2nd Division 46, 52, 67, 78, 88
 3rd Army 11, 12, 13, 26, 37, 39, 41, 58, **58**, **60–62**, 63, **68–70**, 71, 79, 85
 3rd Division 15, 47, 76
 4th Army 11, 25, 26, 37, 40, 41, 47, 57, 66–67, 72, 78, 79
 4th Division 72, 76
 5th (Yalu) Army 15, 24, 26, 37, 40–41, 44, 47, 49, 52, 67, **68–70**, 71, 78
 5th Division 15, **63**, 64, 72, 74–75, 84
 6th Division 81, 84, 85
 7th Division 58, 63–64, 72, 76, 80, 84, 85
 8th Division 15, **18**, 64, 72, 74–75
 9th Division 58, 63–64, 65, 66, 72, 73, 76, 80, 81
 9th Kobi Brigade 44, 46
 10th Division 26, 67, 76
 11th Division 15, 41, 44, 46, 49, 53, 76, 85, 90
 12th Division 47, 52, 53, 67, 88
 Guards Division 47, 52, 53, 67, 81, 85, 87
Imperial Japanese Navy 10, 91
Imperial Russian Army **39**
 artillery **19**, 28, 30–31, **31**
 cavalry 5, 13–14, **13**, **14**, 31, 88
 commanders 22–23, **23**, 24
 Cossacks 47, 52, 58, **60–62**, 78, 80
 defensive systems 28–29, **28**, **29**
 failure 90
 final mobilization waves 89–90
 line of supply 27, 38–39, **38**
 officers 4–5, 27
 order of battle 34–36
 organization 29–30
 quality 27–28, **28**
 reserve system 27–28
 shortcomings 4–5
 stocism **75**
 strength 6, 8, 10, 11, 27, 36, 89
 transformation 4–5
 uniforms **4**, **13**, **27**, **66**, **67**
 weapons 30
Imperial Russian Army formations
 1st Manchurian Army 5, 18–19, 23, 29, 30, 31, 34, 39, 43, 44, 47, 52, 71, 79, 88
 1st Siberian Corps 11, 15, 18, 19, 28, 30, 35, 47, 65, 67, 71, 74, 76, 85
 1st Trans-Baikal Cossack Battery **60–62**
 2nd Manchurian Army 13, 18–19, 23, 24, 29, 31, 35, 39, 47, 58, **58**, **60–62**, 63, 63–64, 66,

72, 73, 75, 79–80, 81, 84, 85, 87–88, 88
3rd Manchurian Army 18, 18–19, 24, 29, 35–36, 39, 40, 57, 66, 72, 79, 85, 87–88, 88
3rd Siberian Corps 11, 28, 34, 47, 52
4th Siberian Corps 34, 57, 81
4th Ural Cossack Regiment 58, 63
5th East Siberian Rifle Regiment 10
5th Siberian Corps 35, 72, 76
5th Ural Cossacks 58, **60–62**
6th Siberian Corps **29**, 36, 39, 76
25th Division 65, 66
72nd Division 39, 75
Chenghocheng Detachment 24, 34–35, 43, 44, 46, 47, 49, 67, **68–70**, 71
Chernoyar Regiment **68–70**
General Reserve 34, 46, 47, 53, 63, 65
I Corps 34, 39, 57
VIII Corps 15, 18, 35
X Corps 15, 35, 65–66
XVI Corps 34, 39
XVII Corps 24, 57, 85
XVIII Corps 35–36
Imperial Russian Navy, Russian Pacific Squadron 8

Japanese Empire, rise of 6, 7–8
Japanese General Staff 31

Kao-li-ma **60–62**
Kaulbars, General Aleksandr Vasilievich 19, 23–24, 35, 39, 46, 58, 63–64, 64, 65–66, 66, 71, 73, 74–75, 76
Kawamura, General Kageaki 15, 26, 37, 40–41, 46, 47, 49, 52, 53, 67, 78
Keller, Feodor 11, **11**
Khoranov, Colonel 14
Kodama, General 41
Kuroki, General Tametomo 10, 11, 25, **25**, 26, 36, 40, 46, 47, 49, 52, 53, 67, 76, 78, 79, 88
Kuropatkin, Aleksey Nikolaevich 4, 5, 11, 22–23, **23**, 29, 34, 43
  automobile 40
  Battle for Mukden 81
  Battle of San-de-pu 15, 18–19
  counter-attack on the Western Flank 71–72, 73, 74, 75, 76
  deployment 25 February 47
  at Mukden 24, 46, 52, 53
  Nogi's envelopment 63, 64–65, 66
  orders retreat to the Hun-Ho 75, 78
  personal command 39
  plan 38–39, **38**
  prioritization of the east 63
  removal from command 88
  retreat from Mukden 84, 85, 87–88
  retreat to Mukden 12, 79, 80
Kursk, Grand Manoeuvres, 1902: 4, 5, 8

Liaoyang 10, 11, 12, 24, 25, 26, 28
Linevich, General Nikolai Petrovich 23, **23**, 34, 44, 46, 47, 49, 52, 53, 67, 71, 75, 78, 79, 81, 84–85, 85, 87–88, 89, 90, 91
logistics 12
Lüshunkou (later Port Arthur) 7

machine guns 8, **10**, 18, 28, 30, 32–33, **32**, 44, 52, 64, **68–70**
Manchurian theatre 7, 7–8, **9**, 86
Mishchenko, Pavel 13–14, 43
Mishchenko's cavalry raid 13–15, **13**
modern combat, characteristics of 90–91
Motien Pass, Battle of 11, **11**, 24
Muilov, Lt Gen 80, 80–81, 81, 84, 85
Mukden 42, **85**, 87, 92–93, **92**, **93**
  Battle for 31, 80–81, **82–83**, 84–85, **84**, **85**, 87, 90
  defensive positions 12
  retreat from 84, 84–85, **84**, 85, 87–88
  Russian evacuation 81, 84
  Russian retreat to 12, 78–80
  strategic importance 10
Mukden Incident, 1933: 93

Nanshan, Battle of 10
Newchuang 13, 14
Nicholas II, Tsar 7, 19, 89
Nodzu, General Michitsura 11, 25–26, 37, 40, 41, 57, 66–67, 72, 76, 78, 79, 88
Nogi, General Maresuke 10–11, 12, 13, 14–15, 26, **26**, 37, 39, 41, 43, 47, 58, 63, 72–73, 73, 74–75, 75–76, 79–80, 81, 85, 87
Novgorod Hill 42, 57

Oku, General Yasukata 10–11, 11, 18, **18**, 25–26, 36–37, 41, 63, 64, 65–66, 72, 73–74, 76, 79–80, 81, 84, 88
Oyama, Field Marshal Iwao 11, 12, 13, 14, 24–25, **25**, 26, 32, 87
  aggressive approach 91
  Battle of San-de-pu 15, 18, 19
  diversionary attack 41
  minimal approach 40
  at Mukden 47, 71
  Nogi's envelopment 63
  plan 40–41

Russian counter-attack on the Western Flank 71–73

Palmer, Frederick 25
Port Arthur 8, 10, 11, 25
  Russian surrender 12, 12–13, 26
  siege of 11, 12, 26
Putilov Hill 42, **43**, 57, 67, 78
Pyongyang 10

railways 6, 7, 8, 10, **13**, 14, 27, 38, **38**, 71, 90
remembrance 93
Rennenkampf, Pavel (Paul) Karlovich von 24, **24**, 31, 34, 43, 47, 49, 52, 53, 67, **68–70**, 71, 76, 78, 84–85, 85, 87–88, 90
Rennenkampf Hill 46
Russian Empire 6–8, **7**, 90
Russian War Ministry 6
Russo-Japanese War
  1904-January 1905 8, **9**, 10-12
  end of 91
  Japanese plans 10
  road to 6–8
Russo-Turkish War 4, 5, 22, 23, 24, 27

San-de-pu, Battle of 13, **13**, 15, **15**, **16–17**, 18–19, **18**, **19**, 24, 30, 93
Sha-Ho River 42, 57, 71, 75, 92–93
  Battle of the **11**, 12, 24, 25, 26
Sha-lin-pu, fight at 65
Sino-Japanese War 7, 25, 26, 31
Soloviev, Captain L. Z. 30, 33, 90
Stackelberg, Gen Georg von 11
Stoessel, Gen Anatoly 12

tactics 29, 30, 31, **32**
technological developments 8, 23, 29
Telissu, Battle of 11
terrain 42, **42**, 53, 65
theatre of war **6**
Tieh-ling 80, 87, 88
Trans-Siberian Railway 6, 7, 8, 27, 38, **38**, 89
Tsai-yen-tzu, action at 65
Tserpitski, Lt Gen 73, 74–75, 85
Tsushima, Battle of 91
Tu-pin-tai 49

von der Launitz, Gen 65, 66, 72, 73, 76, 79–80, 80–81, 84, 85

weather 18, 44, 64
Witte, Sergei 6, 7

Yalu river 10, 25, 28